Families Communicating with Children

To Stephanie and Paul – I am incredibly proud of you both and ever thankful for your help in my parental communication development. T. J. S.

To Mike, Terry, Ray, and Pat for the lessons only siblings can teach, and for the joys of aunthood. J. Y.

Families Communicating with Children

Building Positive Developmental Foundations

Thomas J. Socha and Julie Yingling

polity

First published in 2010 by Polity Press

Polity Press
65 Bridge Street
Cambridge CB2 1UR, UK

Polity Press
350 Main Street
Malden, MA 02148, USA

ISBN-13: 978-0-7456-4612-1 (hardback)
ISBN-13: 978-0-7456-4613-8 (paperback)

A catalogue record for this book is available from the British Library.

Typeset in 11 on 13 pt Sabon
by Servis Filmsetting Ltd, Stockport, Cheshire
Printed and bound by MPG Books Group, UK

The publisher has used its best endeavors to ensure that the URLs for external websites referred to in this book are correct and active at the time of going to press. However, the publisher has no responsibility for the websites and can make no guarantee that a site will remain live or that the content is or will remain appropriate.

Every effort has been made to trace all copyright holders, but if any have been inadvertently overlooked the publisher will be pleased to include any necessary credits in any subsequent reprint or edition.

For further information on Polity, visit our website: www.politybooks.com

Contents

Preface

There is widespread agreement that we live in the age of communication and that effective communication is critical for success. There is also widespread agreement that families' communication with children from birth to age 5 creates the foundation upon which future communication development is built. Thus, if we as a society are serious about improving communication effectiveness, we must pay close attention to the foundations of communication learning at home, as well as monitor the trajectory of communication growth and learning across the human lifespan.

Each year thousands of students in the US and beyond take undergraduate and graduate courses in family communication, but unfortunately many will end these courses with an incomplete understanding of family communication. Why? Because most family communication courses do not provide an adequate understanding of children's communication and its development at home. Also, today, most graduate programs in family communication do not require students to develop an understanding of children's communication, or if they do, students take classes offered outside the communication field in developmental psychology or education. In fact, as this book is published, the field of communication does not have a children's communication book in print. There are historical reasons for this state of affairs.

The discipline of communication formed by splintering away, first from English departments, as rhetoric, and then from various social sciences, as when interpersonal communication arose from psychology, and group communication from social psychology and sociology. Although these social sciences, especially psychology, continue to try to explain children's development, the same cannot be said about communication studies. Beginning with its earliest studies of spoken persuasion and relational communication, the communication field has studied mostly adults. This may be because of difficulties inherent in researching children, difficulties in gaining access to children as research participants, and so on, but it could also be the communication field's failure to appreciate that when we study adults' communication we are actually studying the result of something that took many years to develop.

When an 18-year-old college freshman gives a speech in a public speaking class many developmental factors have influenced the student's performance long before the speech. Some factors can be traced to school-based communication learning that took place while giving previous "speeches" in other classes, but family-based communication learning also should be considered. Besides exposure to school speaking experiences (in grades K-12), did the student's parents model and encourage animated storytelling during dinners? Did they create a supportive communication climate that allowed children to speak freely at home? Was positive feedback given when children spoke about their experiences at home? Were children encouraged to tell about their experiences? Were children included and encouraged to debate during dinners? If we are to better understand communication, we need to better understand its origins as well as the factors that affect its development across contexts. An important goal of this book is to help you to begin to think developmentally about communication: Where did a particular communication skill start? Upon what kind of foundation was the communication skill built? What happened as it developed? And, what might change its future development?

Historically, with the exception of research about television and children (e.g. see Van Evra, 2004), studies about children's communication represent a relatively small and unnoticed area outside the mainstream of communication scholarship. Children's communication studies are also scattered widely throughout the communication literature (making it difficult to sketch a broad picture of the state of this work) and many excellent studies that shed light on the development of particular communication skills were conducted decades ago: person-centered communication (e.g. Delia & Clark, 1977), persuasive skills (e.g. Delia, Kline, & Burleson, 1979), emotional support skills (e.g. Burleson & Kunkel, 1996), and others. And, over the past thirty years, only three textbooks were published on children's communication (e.g. Haslett & Samter, 1997; Hopper & Naremore, 1978; Wood, B. S., 1981). Today, none are in print.

It was not until the mid 1990s, as family communication began to come into its own as a specialty within the communication field, that communication scholars began to realize that we cannot fully examine family life, nor fully understand human communication development across the lifespan, without considering how children both influence and are influenced in families (e.g. see Socha & Stamp, 1995).

For students, this textbook begins to fill this gap in family communication education in two ways. First, it provides an introduction to children's communication within families by presenting both classic, foundational ideas about human development and more recent research about communication from birth through late childhood. Students will find that communication changes across the lifespan and that age makes for huge differences in communication skill. Second, it offers a new, positive perspective from which to view children's communication at home. A positive approach to family communication focuses on the communication processes that create optimal conditions for the development of human capacities. This approach also assumes that humans continue to develop across their lifespan, and that families are the social groupings most able and willing to nurture that development.

For family communication scholars and graduate students, this book also calls attention to the need for courses in children's communication, for graduate students of family communication to specialize in children, and for family communication scholars to make the study of children's communication a priority in research and education. It is our hope that the communication discipline will remember that children are family communicators too.

About the Authors

The authors of this book have been studying children and families for most of their careers. In the late 1970s, Tom studied children's communication with Professor Barbara S. Wood during his MA program in Communication at the University of Illinois at Chicago. Professor Wood authored one of the communication field's most widely used textbooks on children's communication. During his Ph.D. program at the University of Iowa, Tom took courses that focused on families, children, and human development outside the communication department (in the departments of counselor education, home economics, psychology, religious studies, social work, and sociology) as well as taught the first undergraduate course in family communication in the Communication Department at the University of Iowa (with fellow communication graduate student, Robert Martin). Since 1989, at Old Dominion University, Tom has been teaching a course in family communication, and in 1991 began teaching a course on children's communication. His children's communication course is an upper undergraduate– beginning graduate communication elective that is also taken as an elective in an interdisciplinary course cluster called "The World of Children" (that includes courses from Criminal Justice, Education, English, Psychology, and Sociology). Tom has published research examining children's group communication, children's humor, families communicating about race, as well as co-edited (with Professor Glen Stamp, Ball State University) the communication field's first edited volume on parent–child communication. He was the founding editor of the *Journal of Family Communication* (2000–2005) and recently co-edited the communication field's first book to examine parents and children communicating in relationships outside of home (Socha & Stamp, 2009).

Julie did her undergraduate work in sociology and anthropology with a smattering of psychology – all the human sciences she could find at the time. While working at the University of Denver, she discovered Frank Dance's courses in Psychology of Speech Communication and became fascinated with the question of how we come to communicate as we do. Her dissertation on infant speech required coursework and mentors in related departments, notably speech science and psychology. She subsequently taught such courses as Psychology of Communication and Communication Development, among others (e.g. Health Communication, Relational Communication, Communication Theory), at the University of Wisconsin-Milwaukee, the University of Northern Colorado, Humboldt State University and the University of Iowa. Publications have included research reports on infant–parent interaction, children's friendships, and children's communication needs when in treatment for cancer. In the year she chose to retire, her lifespan development text saw print. Since then, she has also co-authored a book about final conversations with dying loved ones. With Professor Maureen Keeley, Julie is preparing a final conversations book for children who have experienced the death of a close family member.

1

Children are Family Communicators too

Family life can be a source of our greatest joy and deepest pain. There will be times for each of us when we seek to embrace the power of family, and times when we seek to escape its influence. The joy and pain of family life may be simultaneous. During the several days following her father's death, Julie experienced the joy of family support and memories as well as the pain of deep, shared grief. We all also try to make sense of family life. Some individuals spend thousands of dollars and many hours in counseling attempting to probe family's depths, while others are content to experience its daily ebb and flow at the surface.

There is widespread agreement that family's influence on human development is broad, complex, and stretches across the human lifespan. And given family's influence, it is clear that to thrive we must develop greater mindfulness about family communication dynamics, paying special attention to early family life: the foundation of future development.

For students of communication, the family is variously defined as a special small group, a system of caring interpersonal relationships, a unique organization, or an informal classroom. It is inherently fascinating because we all experience "family," yet each in a unique fashion. We develop personal and shared meanings for "family" that are often resistant to change. As you study families, you may find it easy to understand how the families of others change with time, counseling, or crisis; yet also find it very difficult to observe possibilities for change in your own family. Why?

1

Because we create, share, and maintain our symbols, our methods for understanding ourselves and everything else in the context of our families. Consequently, we develop blind spots that prevent us from seeing our own families fully, and we perceive through lenses that may distort our view of the many good (and bad) things of family life. If you have viewed *Charlie and the Chocolate Factory* (an adult version of a child's story) you may recall Johnny Depp's portrayal of Willy Wonka as a child-man whose definition of family is very negative and is based on his experiences with a stern and unforgiving father. His surprise and confusion is considerable when he discovers that Charlie's definition is positive and warm, as it is linked to a close and loving extended family. Consider your own definition of family; it may differ considerably from that of your friends' definitions. Yet you each were nurtured and you each developed, albeit with different outcomes.

Families vary, not just individually, but structurally and culturally. Some families have two parents, or multiple parents, either at one time (polygamy) or at different times and locations (serial monogamy, sometimes resulting in multiple step-parents). Some families are related by blood and others by consensual bonds of affection and support. Some are limited to parents and their offspring while others extend beyond genetic links to communal life. But the one common element across all families is their **developmental** character.

Development is what families do; it is a primary reason for their being. This is true not only for procreative families (families birthing and raising children), but for families of all sorts. Indeed, development is not something that just happens in early family life; development continues across the entire human lifespan. And family is the incubator for human development.

Family communication scholars continue to define "family" in ways that reflect increasing inclusiveness and complexity, and many definitions of family mention it as a lifespan group (Socha, 1999). For example, according to Turner and West (2002):

Family is a self-defined group of intimates who create and maintain themselves through their own interactions and their interactions with

2

others; a family may include both voluntary and involuntary relationships; it creates both literal and symbolic internal and external
boundaries; and it evolves through time: It has a history, a present,
and a future. (p. 9)

The idea that families evolve (or change) over time is rather obvious.
Your family of today is not the same as a decade ago. However, it is
important to understand that families can facilitate or inhibit their
changes over time. Since development is inherently future-oriented,
we find it useful to think of **family** as a nexus of individuals linked
by consent or birth who collaborate in the creation and continuation of family identity and in the development of the potentialities
of the system, its relationships, and its members (adapted from
Socha, 2006). Families use communication to create conditions for
the development of many capacities on multiple levels (individual,
relational, group) (Socha, 2006; 2009). So, to understand family
communication and to assess its outcomes, we must also understand how development proceeds and how family relationships
both affect and are affected by developmental processes.

Thinking about families as a nexus of intimates charged with
potential-development is also a positive way to focus attention
on two facets of that agency: the communication processes that
facilitate the growth of human potential and the construction of
communication resources to manage obstacles inhibiting development. So, instead of focusing primarily on family communication
problems and how to fix them, we choose to focus on the dual
roles of family communication in developing eloquent, artful, and
exciting communicators, and in building family communication
resources that prevent and manage obstacles in the path of positive communication development. Following the lead of positive
psychologists, we call this a **positive approach** to family communication as its primary focus is on creating optimal conditions for
development. A positive approach does not mean that all family
communication is bright and cheery, but rather that the kinds
of communication processes that contribute to the development
of adaptive (successful) capacities and relationships are supportive of mutually agreed upon 'positive' outcomes. However,

we should also remember that we all have somewhat different ideas of what family is, and what kinds of "positive outcomes" families seek to accomplish. Positive outcomes are in the eye of the beholder and require some negotiation among members, although certain individual character strengths (being honest, valuing learning, appreciating beauty, and so on) seem universally admired (Peterson & Seligman, 2004).

Human Development: Causes and Outcomes

As with all living things, children grow – they get bigger with time. Not only that, they **mature** – their bodies change in both form and function. But further, humans develop communication capacities, thought processes, complex emotions, and skill sets that are not simply results of growth and maturation. They are, to some extent, self-constructed, but always on the basis of sensory input and the support of interacting others – often, family.

As we explain the basics of human development and how it proceeds from birth through early childhood, you will notice that some sources we use may date back years. These sources are foundational works that are significant in understanding the role of communication in development. As we examine communication specifics, we will also add recent research that builds upon these classic foundations. In this book we also concentrate on communication development and young children: from birth to about ages 7–10. Given the scope and depth of information available about adolescence and page limitations of this volume, we will only touch on family communication during adolescence, and pay primary attention to young children. Further, when information about the timing of development of particular communication skills and abilities is available and supported by research we will note it. However, timing communication's development is not an exact science as there are individual differences as well as contextual factors that affect developmental arcs. We do, however, include a communication development chart in Chapter 2 that offers a general picture of "what to expect when."

What Causes Human Development?

Historical explanations for human development divided into two camps: nature and nurture. The **nativists** argue that we become human entirely as a result of physiological maturation. Today, few strict nativists remain, but some who have made strong arguments for biological bases of human behaviors continue to be influential, such as linguist Noam Chomsky (e.g. Chomsky, 1965) and his student, Stephen Pinker, who attribute human communicative and cognitive abilities to innate brain structure, originally dubbed the Language Acquisition Device (LAD). In the communication field, "Communibiology" (e.g. see Beatty & McCroskey, 2000) presents the less rigid view that physiological systems may strongly influence communication behavior. In general, nativists argue for various kinds of universal human effects. In Chomsky's case, it is for a "universal grammar" of topic-and-comment (i.e. subject-and-verb) language structure. For Beatty and McCroskey it is for universal communication adaptability – the capacity to adjust to social situations. They conclude, for example, that wit and social composure are probably inherited tendencies. Indeed, wit as a component of intelligence, and social composure as a component of temperament, are likely to be affected by genetics. But there is much more to our behavior that is not.

On the other side of the coin, and also rare, are scholars who take the view that nurture, or environmental effects, are solely responsible for our behavior. Strict **behaviorists**, such as B. F. Skinner (1974) viewed human infants as "blank slates" who soak up the surrounding reality by a form of conditioning, à la Pavlov's dogs' salivating response to a bell when paired with food. What Skinner failed to note was that Pavlov's explanation of human behavior went much further to posit a "second signal system" specific to humans over and above the "first signal system" manipulated in Pavlov's dogs (Pavlov, 1928–41). Chomsky's argument against strict behaviorism was that a five-year-old human would need more years than humans have populated Earth to develop their normal linguistic sophistication by simple conditioning. Regardless of the impossibility of

5

proving such a statement, others agreed with his basic premise. And they were not all nativists.

The new **interactionists** were scholars like Jerome Bruner (1975) who posited that we must look to both nature and nurture to explain fully how humans come to communicate and think as they do. Bruner, while admitting that humans have a specialized brain, a sort of LAD, claimed that they also must have LASS, or a language acquisition support system, to develop normal human behavior. He observed infants and parents interacting and noted that parents with their babies act as though they are interacting with a fully functioning human. Furthermore, infants, though without speech, interact to the fullest of their abilities with parents. And gradually, their behavior begins to approximate adult interaction.

A later interactionist from psychology, Alan Fogel (1993), claimed that "individuals develop through their relationships with others" (p. 3). He disagreed with Chomsky in that he accounted for developmental changes in everyday communication rather than in some "inaccessible area of the brain or the cell" (p. 5). Fogel's concept of **co-regulation** is a useful one to describe the creative process of joint action that is the "fundamental source of developmental change" (p. 6).

In the communication field, most scholars who study inter-personal and developmental communication are interactionists of some stripe. John Shotter (1993) who called his form of interactionism "social constructionism," theorized that self, rela-tionships, and our understandings of reality are all created in joint transactions. If he is right then most of our foundational meanings including the sense of self are constituted in early transactions with those most available: family members.

For most social scientists, human behavior cannot be explained adequately by "nature" alone or simply by processes of growth and maturation. Beyond the necessary endowments of a brain capacity for combining chunks of information and a sound-making capacity for producing maximally distinct sounds, humans need other humans to begin constructing meanings. The process of sense-making was explained by Piaget (1959), the father of developmental psychology, as the result of opposing functions of assimilation and accommodation. **Assimilation** involves taking in information from an external environment, while **accommodation** occurs by changing the internal system to adapt to information that doesn't quite fit into the present system. The process of learning about others and the world occurs first in interaction external to oneself – at one's periphery – and that assimilation then must be integrated (accommodated) to one's core, thus changing the sense-making system.

Shotter (1993) considered this construction of meaning, at the place where two humans' peripheries meet, the "zone of uncertainty about who can do what in the construction of a word's significance" (p. 125). That meeting is the point of power where two people try to shape a social reality in the frontier between them. Not only is a relationship built, but meanings are adjusted for both. And in children, meanings must first be created and later adapted. For instance, 2-year-old Leah learns the word "justice" during a trip to the courthouse with her mom to pay a traffic fine and associates the word with the building and the people in it. At 7, she adds meaning from a teacher's unit on civil rights. By the age of 14, she is savvy enough about the broad and multiple meanings of "justice" that she uses it in an argument with her parents about curfew. All the contexts in which she used the word with more sophisticated communicators inform her meaning for the word. Human development – of meaning, of sophisticated cognition, of identity, of communicative skills and relationships – relies on social interaction.

What Develops?

What develops that moves humans beyond sheer growth to the constitution of particularities associated with our species? The answer seems to reside in our rather odd (compared to the rest of earth's creatures) way of communicating. We certainly share some communication modes with other animals similar to us, mammals and especially primates. We grin, we scratch, we howl occasionally. Those are all forms of **communication**: "that which links any organism together" (Cherry, 1966, p. 36). But those forms seem to pale in significance for us once we begin to use **spoken language,** which arises from an innate capacity to articulate speech and to process distinctive sounds produced by interacting with others.

To put it simply, humans are genetically endowed not only to hear a variety of sounds distinctly, but to understand them as sequentially related patterns. This, even infants can do, but other primates cannot. Humans share with their closest relatives an ability to recognize sound patterns holistically, but the identification of the pattern components and their sequential order is limited to humans (Warren & Ackroff, 1976). What this means is that we can parse the sounds of a sentence into components and use not only the sounds but their **syntax,** or ordering, to understand its meaning. So, for example, the sentence, "Jan grew past the height of the ivy trellis," is composed of quite a few distinctive sounds which, if ordered differently, also could mean something quite different, as in "The height of the trellis passed the ivy Jan grew." The maximum number of distinct sounds that other primates can keep in proper order appears to be three; ours is nearly limitless (Warren & Ackroff, 1976). Our brains are not set up willy-nilly to handle complicated input; they are set up to handle the kinds of distinctive sounds we produce. We articulate sounds that are distinctive enough to tell one from the next in a rapid sequence, and our two brain hemispheres function differently so as to assign meaning and order to the sequence. So, human communication is, at least in its normal inception, spoken and symbolic. Infants begin to produce articulated sound at around 6 months of age and, with the impetus of interaction, begin to load meaning onto those sounds (for example, "dada" said in a questioning tone can come to mean, "is that daddy?"). By 18 months, they are using combinations of sounds that are recognizably symbolic and syntactic (now, the child can say more specifically, "dada come home?").

The time between birth and toddlerhood is critical for the development of human communication. Apparently, sometime in that period, children must hear others interacting symbolically, and try to participate themselves, or they may fail to realize the promise of the **symbol.** Symbols are the building blocks for language; they are ways to represent things, ideas, and emotions. Let's take the example of the infant's word: "dada." When it is first used, it probably was one of the simplest sounds for the infant to produce and it is used simply to reference an experience, typically "interaction with dad," or "play time with the guy" or "here comes that fun male again." This is not symbolic yet, because it is tied to concrete experience. But, by the age of 5, when the child uses the word "dad" she could mean any number of things, depending on the linguistic context ("Loren's dad picked us up" when arriving at home) and the situation ("I miss my Dad when he travels" when with caring friends). Symbols bear no real, concrete relationship to the thing they represent, but instead are arbitrarily selected to bear meaning (in this case, a type of relationship). They may be, and often are, sounds, but can also be gestures, visual representations and so forth (a "d" drawn in the air, a sketch). But speech is the stimulus that seems to send us searching for meaning.

Suzanne Langer (1972), in discussing the "great shift" to symbols in human evolution, noted that "speech is a process which has created an instrument, language" (p. 297). Speech is a natural birthright, which leads us to language, which leads us to multiple effects on thinking, feeling, and interacting. One of the most instructive examples of the "discovery" of symbols by an individual is Helen Keller's story.

Helen was introduced to human interaction in the usual familial context but then, at around eighteen months, suffered an illness that took both her sight and her hearing. Although she may have experienced the beginning stages of symbol development, she did not complete it until many years later, when as an 8-year-old, Helen walked to the well with her new teacher, Annie Sullivan. Ms Sullivan had tried everything she knew to fill in the blanks left by Helen's sensory loss, but had little success. The child was wild, willful, and merely responded to commands as a well-trained animal would. But at the well, Annie tried something new. Placing one of Helen's hands under the cool water, she spelled the signs for "w-a-t-e-r" into the other. Many years later, the then very literate and educated Helen reported her memory of that moment: "Suddenly I felt a misty consciousness as of something forgotten – a thrill of returning thought; and somehow the mystery of language was revealed to me.

I knew then that "w-a-t-e-r" meant the wonderful cool something that was flowing over my hand. . . . I left the well-house eager to learn. Everything had a name, and each name gave birth to a new thought" (Keller, as quoted in Percy, 1954, pp. 34–35).

Another stunning example of a child who did not symbolize during that early critical period is Genie. However, it was not deafness that deprived her, it was isolation. Genie was found at the age of 13, confined in a small room in a Los Angeles suburb. She looked half her age and did not speak or respond to speech. Genie's mother was completely cowed by her husband who forbade her to interact with Genie. And he merely growled at his daughter occasionally. Thus, she heard no normal human interaction until she was 13 – past the critical period for acquiring language. Genie subsequently received care from psychologists and doctors as well as training from a linguist. But Genie, although she began to use sounds to refer to things, never really mastered syntax and thus never was able to engage fully in everyday human interaction (Curtiss, 1977). It was Genie's isolation that kept her from recognizing the power of spoken symbolic communication at the right time. In the normal course of family communication, Genie would have interacted with caring family members and acquired language naturally. In Helen's case, she lost the genetic gift to hear speech; in Genie's, she was deprived of the interaction environment. Helen was fortunate to have Ms Sullivan bring back the hazy memory of symbolic meaning.

So both interaction and speech are necessary to human communication. Genetics provides most humans with the capacity for speech (to hear and produce articulate sound), but the family most often provides early interaction opportunities. And many human behaviors and characteristics proceed from spoken symbolic interaction.

What are the Outcomes of Developing Spoken Symbols?

The ability to use symbols gives us the raw material to build thought processes we would not otherwise construct. The process of discovering symbols may run something like this: The baby

10

begins to use a particular sound ("baba") to represent a particular experience (receiving his bottle). This simple **representation** is something primates and probably some other mammals can also do, such as link a particular gesture or sound with an object or experience (i.e. when I say "walk" in any context, as in "Let's take a walk tomorrow," my dog heads to the door immediately). The next stage is **categorization,** when the sound's meaning becomes extended to refer to all instances of a particular category ("baba" refers now to any liquid receptacle that Sam sees; e.g. bottle, cup, mug, vase). Some scholars of animal behavior believe that dolphins and primates may be capable of categorization (linking the mug in your hand with the icon on a card showing a bottle). However, the crux of symbolizing lies in **differentiation,** when the symbol is used to contrast one meaning to another ("baba" now has a specialized meaning, something like "enclosed liquid holder"). Sam can now contrast "x" against "not-x" (i.e. a bottle is not a cup/mug/plate/ walrus) and that provides the foundation for building concepts (see Chapter 2 of this volume). A related development is the use of **negation**. This has a clear beginning when the child delights in saying "NO" to anything and everything. The ability to negate is a powerful resource. As far as we know, only humans can conceive of something that does not exist. The repercussions for imagination and creativity, as well as for deceit, are unending. But in terms of the next developmental step, it is the contrast between "me" and "not-me" that is of interest.

Individuation begins to occur when the self can be felt as separate from the primary other, usually mother or father. We could discuss this development as the first source of existential angst or separation anxiety, but it is also the first step toward self-awareness and identity. And it is the beginning of **egocentrism,** or the inability to conceive of any view but one's own. Typically, psychologists view this as an early stage in development, but that is not to say that older humans never experience it. Indeed there is a recognized stage of "secondary egocentrism" (Elkind, 1974) in adolescence that accounts for certain teenaged behaviors. In young babies, it is a fixedness of view that is restricted to the child's own experience of the world. Jean Piaget (1959) explained **egocentric** speech as the side effect of egocentric thinking; he believed it faded away as children approached school age. More about this will be found below.

Socialization begins with bridging the gap in meaning between self and other. It might start when the infant becomes mightily frustrated with not being able to signal what he wants from the parent. Early on, empathy and instinct will suffice as mother recognizes what the infant's discomfort is (wet diaper) or reacts to her baby's hunger needs (with the let-down of her milk). But as the child's needs become more complex, things get dicier. If little Max has developed a taste for bananas and there is a bowl full of various fruits on the table, he may reach for it and grunt. Mind you, Mom recognizes he wants *something* in that direction but which *something*, she can only guess. If, instead of picking up each piece and offering it until he takes one, she waits through a few of his attempts, then she is prodding him to develop a way of interacting that takes her into account. If she names each piece ("apple," "kiwi," "banana") as she touches them, she gives him a chance to signal great interest in one. And, she provides him with the sound he will want to try to produce. Gradually, as he develops further, he will be able to **decenter** or to see things from mother's point of view (i.e. that she cannot know which he wants unless he specifies). Max will begin to realize that Mom, in the absence of fruit to point to, does not have the same banana-image going for her that he sees so clearly when hungry. So, he learns that "nana" will lead her to see the banana-image too.

Socialized speech begins later, as children are able to think about how to address certain others in view of their particular needs. Consider 2-year-old Mabel and her 7-year-old sister Daisy. They have both entered the house around 4:30 p.m., after playing tag. Mom is cooking dinner and the girls are hungry. Mabel blurts out: "I want a banana!" while Daisy considers: Mom cooking dinner, the time of day, and her desires. She says quietly: "Mom, if you give me a banana now, I'll eat my broccoli at dinner." Her message was adapted for her mother and the situation, and if Mabel were not standing right there, Daisy probably would get the banana, or at least half.

12

Piaget (1959) observed that such socialized speech picks up where egocentric speech leaves off, somewhere around the age of 7. He concluded that egocentric speech served no purpose except to produce discomfort that would spur the child to a more socialized speech. However, Lev Vygotsky (1934/1986) considered Piaget's explanation insufficient; he suspected that egocentric speech served a purpose and was not simply a stage on the way to socialized speech. He performed his own observations of children completing more and more difficult tasks, and came to different conclusions.

Vygotsky found that the use of egocentric speech increased with the difficulty of the task he gave them. For example, if a boy is given the box of crayons and told to draw his house, he may occasionally say something like, "I'm drawing my house. Here's the window." But if a color or two is removed from the box, the speech is more frequent, such as "Where's the green crayon? I need the green crayon for the grass. Oh, well, I'll use blue and wet it to make it darker." Here was Vygotsky's interpretation: the child is using egocentric speech to solve problems for himself. He cannot yet *think* to himself in symbols; he must say them out loud. So, egocentric speech is speech for his own purposes, spoken aloud at first, and then gradually (between about 2 and 7) internalized to be used silently – mentally – to direct his behavior. Later, we will look at how the problem-solving process is transformed, once it is internalized, to serve learning and analytic thought.

Internalization is a description of thinking from the outside in; a process of bringing in experience to an already mentally functioning core where the experience may be stored in symbols and restructured for further use, affecting the established sense-making system. For the very young child, a new kind of thought is formed from the raw material of symbols. As Langer (1972) put it: "A genuine symbol is, above all, an instrument of conception and cannot be said to exist short of meeting that requirement" (p. 289). It is in this transformation from speech used for simple reference to true spoken symbols that our capacities to plan, dream, and create emerge, but not in a vacuum. We interact not only to *express* our sense-making but we interact to *construct* meaning

13

together by way of symbols we share. For Vygotsky, human mental functions are "psychological tools" that are the products of symbolic interaction (Kozulin, in Vygotsky, 1934/1986, p. xxiv). In the next chapter, we will look more closely at how these human mental functions are built.

The Family as Developmental

For us, the family is a set of intimate relationships, a nexus of participants that collaborate to create conditions for emerging capacities, such as communication skills, intellectual processes, emotional expression, social strategies, spiritual depth, and artistic performance. The character and quality of those relationships influence all members in the family, but they especially influence children. Children learn to speak, think, and feel in their family environments. They develop a sense of self (identity) and sense of others (relationships) that evolve over a lifetime. Thus, children develop primary functions of communication in the context of family that leads to secondary constructions and various kinds of communication outcomes.

Functions of Family Communication

Although there are many more purposes for families (e.g. pro-creation, companionship, safety, security, and so on), Le Poire (2005) suggests that family communication functions in basically two ways: to **nurture** and **control**. Nurturing is something we do primarily, but not exclusively, in families. We nurture our children, our spouses, our parents, by supporting their development and achievements, by providing safety and security and nourishment. The inevitable partner of nurturance is an openness among members that allows for influence or control. We expect our family members to influence us, to have a point of view about us, to expect things of us. And they do. Parents expect to provide structure for their children and give assistance to aging parents. Children expect to persuade their parents and achieve varying degrees of success, as they become more sophisticated communicators. Nurturance provides a platform or foundation for development, while control shapes the direction of development. To the extent that families can provide both a foundation for development and a structure to positively orchestrate and direct behaviors (Socha, 2006), they increase chances of successful, positive outcomes.

Functions of Symbolic Interaction

Dance and Larson (1976) identified three primary functions of spoken symbolic communication: linking, mentation, and regulation. Let's adapt and interpret this trio in light of the similar functions of family communication.

Sociality is apparently the first function to begin to emerge in the newborn. In its embryonic forms, it is similar to the instinctive forms of communication all animals employ. However, there are unique infant behaviors for connecting with their parents that we will explore in the next chapter. Once the child begins to use symbols, sociality becomes more self-directed and purposeful than the early reactive behaviors. Of course, parents' part is to nurture, first by way of bonding between infant and caregiver. And then, it is for family to continue to nurture through the child's egocentrism, through the contrariness of the "terrible twos," and on throughout the various stages of sociality.

Control of others, self, and environment probably begins in the first year with gestures like pointing (to what the baby wants from another), but quickly becomes more sophisticated and successful with words and simple sentences. Much later, skills develop for influence and persuasion. Parents' role in the control function is to provide structure for learning and discipline for optimal behavior, and to be the analytic testing grounds for the development of reasoning and morality.

Cognition, for our purposes, means symbolically mediated thought. It may have its origins in the early use of sounds to recall events or activities. Later, words are spoken aloud to solve problems (egocentric speech) and later, those problem-solving skills are internalized to be performed silently. Then it becomes possible to learn advanced problem-solving skills, or analytic thinking. Parents and siblings are part of this process as well, supporting the process of creative problem-solving by demonstrating thought processes aloud, and challenging the child's developing skills.

Sociality, control, and cognition are primary functions of symbol use and are refined over the course of a lifetime. These three are necessary for the development of other human characteristics, including the secondary constructions of identity and emotion.

Secondary Constructions of Symbolic Interaction

Identity and emotion are but two of many types of symbolic constructs built on the foundation of sociality, control, and cognition. But these two are crucial to human development.

Identity is a developmental process of constituting meaning for the self, based on repeated internalizations of external interactions. Each communicative performance of self builds upon the internalizations that have preceded it. Adjustments are made to identity as interactions serve to affirm or reject the meanings for self already constructed. For example, Sally as a toddler is told she is "Daddy's little beauty" in loving tones. She feels positive about being a girl. She'll add to that foundation later, as being a girl in her social group may come to mean playing with other girls and not with boys. Yet later, she learns behaviors for interacting with boys that she does not use with girls. And so, her gender identity is constructed as she assimilates and accommodates her experience.

Emotions are specific mental states referencing some affective experience, usually performed with symbols. **Affect** is a more general term referencing a range of feelings from simple arousal to symbolic emotion. We begin life with affective experience and continue throughout life with affect, but once we have the use of symbols, we start to imbue our affective experience with symbolic interpretations. Affect generally consists of feeling pleasant or unpleasant, positive or negative. Early responses to affect are generally interest or fear, approach or withdrawal. But responses to emotion are as complex as the emotions themselves. An emotion is distinct from simple affect in that it is characterized by five stages:

(1) it is precipitated by some event or cause, the cause is followed by (2) a negative or positive appraisal, then (3) the physical feeling ensues, along with (4) an expressive response, and finally (5) regulation of self, behavior or action (Planalp, 1999, p.11) which may serve to re-evaluate or accommodate the emotional event.

As children acquire specific symbols for emotions, they become more capable of informing family members of the needs and desires they have formed to suit their developing identities. Sally, for example, may feel rejected when 6-year-old Bart says she "stinks" and she tells her father she feels "bad." Dad, wishing to support her feeling good about her identity, has the option then of giving her words such as "hurt," "frustrated," or "angry" to express how she feels. Sally is given different ways of appraising the situation by those labels, and thus choices of how to respond. If she chooses hurt, she may cry and avoid Bart. If she chooses angry, she may call him a name and gather allies to her. Emotions are all about interpretations of experience.

Communication Outcomes

The outcomes of these primary functions and secondary constructs are relationships, communication strategies, and communication skills. **Relationships** are more or less enduring connections between distinct selves, constructed by both symbolic and non-symbolic interaction. In constructing relationships, we develop expectations and intentions, and set goals. To reach those goals, we must develop strategies and skills. **Strategies** are ways of thinking about problems, in this case, communication problems posed by the pursuit of goals. **Skills** are sets of learned communication behaviors acquired to accomplish interaction goals.

Summary

All families communicate and, in doing so, model for children an array of communication intentions, strategies, and skill sets (e.g. comforting, demonstrating, entertaining, informing, listening, managing conflicts, negotiating, persuading, and more), as well as create and maintain relationships of many kinds (adult–adult, adult–child, child–child, etc.). Of course, the ways families communicate varies a great deal as for example communication in families of varied ethnic cultures (e.g., see Socha & Diggs, 1999, for a discussion about African-American families) and, although the communication literature on this subject is limited, when available we will provide examples of children's cultural communication learning at home. However, some principles of communication and its development apply to all families. One principle that we will emphasize throughout this book is that optimal communication environments that facilitate children's development are created, and parents and caregivers are those who can create them. Further, families that promote optimal communication environments will function smoothly and fulfill the functions of a family successfully.

An optimal learning environment as any educator will tell you is rewarding (positive) rather than punishing (negative) (for a description of the latter, see Kozol, 1992). Therefore, we will be pointing out the contrast between positive and negative communication models and effects. This is not to say that children should be protected from anything but positive outcomes. Children learn best in the "**zone of proximal development**" (Vygotsky, 1978, p. 86) – that space between what children can currently accomplish on their own and what they can achieve with the help of a more mature person. Children learn by reaching for the seemingly impossible, but they are motivated to try by the rewarding positive communication of important others – family members.

The remainder of this text is devoted largely to describing and explaining outcomes of family communication, with particular attention to the outcomes affecting children, as well as the influence of children on family outcomes. We will continue to **bold** important terms throughout the book and include a glossary of their definitions at the end. We hope that you use the glossary as it is an important tool that can help you to acquire the language used in the study of children's communication thereby supporting your comprehension. In the next chapter we will examine how nature and nurture actually break down – what infants bring to the family, and what family provides for the infant.

Activities

1. View one or more of these films: "*L'Enfant Sauvage* (Truffault's 1969 film about the feral "wild boy of Aveyron"), *Genie: Secrets of a Wild Child* (1997 PBS documentary about isolated and neglected Genie), or *The Miracle Worker* (the original 1963 version by Penn may be the best). More recent fictional accounts of "wild children" include *The Secret of Roan Inish* (Sayles' from Columbia, 2000) or *Nell* (Apted's Fox Home, 1994). If you can, compare the documentary with the fictions about isolated children and see what seems true or false about the fiction versions. Then, consider the relative effects of these deficits on human development: What part of human development did these children miss? Did they react differently to their deficits? If you had to choose between profound deafness, complete blindness, or utter isolation for a newborn to suffer, which would have the least effect on the development of normal human abilities?
2. Debate the relative merits of the nature argument or the nurture argument as explanations for human development.
3. Pick a communication skill set at which you are particularly good (e.g. humor, persuasion, listening, comforting, negotiating, and so on) and write a description of how you acquired this skill. From whom did you learn it? How?

Suggested Further Reading

Bruner, J. (1983). *Child's talk: Learning to use language.* New York: Norton.
Gopnik, A., Meltzoff, A. N., & Kuhl, P. K. (1999). *The scientist in the crib: What early learning tells us about the mind.* NY: HarperCollins Publisher.
Vygotsky, L. S. (1978). *Mind in society: The development of higher psychological processes.* Cambridge, MA: Harvard University Press.

2

Children's Communication Development at Home

Most of us cannot remember our first interactions, and it is not because it was so long ago. Voluntary recall is mediated by symbols, so we must have developed meanings for experiences and events to recall them. This does not mean first interactions were unimportant. They are critical for bonding, but also for setting the tone for the child's perception of the world (i.e. as a painful place to be avoided or a pleasurable one to be approached). Although the newborn may interact with many caregivers in the first days, the baby is prepared especially to attend to parents. In this section, we will look at those early endowments for engaging with family members and follow the steps of early development.

Prenatal Sensation for Interaction

Although all our senses develop in utero, only hearing can give useful information about the world outside. True, the fetus often sucks its thumb and probably senses its own body's position in the watery womb, but there isn't sufficient light to see much, and little information to inform a sense of smell. What is left is sound (mother's heartbeat, a muffled voice, a hint of music).

We do know that the acoustic neural pathways are the earliest to **myelinate** before birth (Lecours, 1975). Myelin, a protective sheath that accumulates along nerve fibers to enhance the rapid transmission of neural impulses, forms along acoustic pathways before birth, but continues along other neural paths throughout childhood and for several decades after. Once myelination is complete, the neural impulses travel much faster, but the pathways also become established highways for automatic transmission of information. What we gain in speed and ease, we lose in flexibility of neural connections. Myelination peaks occur at 3 months, 1 year, 5 years, and 15 years when we also see peaks in vocal play, word use, syntax, and abstract thought, respectively. Several of these peaks are considered **critical periods** for language acquisition (Krashen, 1973; Lenneberg, 1967), meaning that certain language milestones must occur at the right time or not at all. Once the maturation of myelin is complete, the pathways for language, and probably other skills as well, cannot be laid down so firmly. Recall that Genie, deprived throughout the critical period for acquiring syntax, never was able to organize language adequately. She did not have the raw material at the right time for building neural pathways for language structure.

The availability of rapid sound reception to the developing fetus may predispose the infant to find the human voice an interesting puzzle (Aslin, 1987). Indeed, expectant mothers who read aloud stories with rhythmic intonation, such as Dr Seuss' *The Cat in the Hat*, subsequently had babies who differentiated between that story and another by Seuss (DeCasper & Spence, 1986). Near-term fetuses also perceive a difference between male and female voices (Lecanuet, Granier-Deferre, Jackquet, Capponi, & Ledru, 1993) thus setting them up aurally to differentiate mother from father. So, infants are predisposed to hear and attend to the human voice, especially ones they have heard prenatally.

Postnatal Sensation for Interaction

The expectant mother and fetus have already begun to establish their bond before birth, but the newborn is then thrust into a world full of sensation. Confronted with unmuffled sound, brightly lit visual displays, sharp smells, and the tactile pressure of being held and moved, newborns often cry and turn away from the "too much" of it. But then, very quickly in healthy neonates, they manage to bring thumb to mouth, to suck and soothe. Healthy infants must be capable not only of withdrawing attention when overwhelmed but of paying close attention to learn about their environment and the people in it (Brazelton, 1973).

Based on the foundation of prenatal audition, newborns hear quite well and seek the sound of a voice. They prefer high-pitched to lower-pitched sounds, probably due to the vagaries of auditory maturation. That preference has the effect of training adults to speak in "motherese" or ACL (adult–child language) that exaggerates the "music" or rhythmic patterns of speech. By one month, and perhaps earlier, infants can distinguish similar human speech sounds, such as the small difference between "pa" and "ba" (Eimas, Siqueland, Jusczyk, & Vigorito, 1971) demonstrating specialized reception for the sounds parents make and the sounds infants must learn to make. Because a newborn has a very large tongue for a very small mouth, and a larynx high enough in the throat to prevent choking, speech production will have to wait. But perception begins to inform the infant about the sounds that will become so important.

Vision, which we come to rely on for information about the world beyond our fingertips, is the least mature of the newborn's senses. Babies are unable to fixate visually until 6 weeks and their focus reaches adult range by about 3 months (Stern, 1977). However, they can fix gaze best on objects about 15 to 18 inches from their faces. And that happens to be the range that adults often choose for face-to-face interaction. Infants are most interested in movement, contrast between light and dark, curved lines rather than straight, and symmetry around a vertical axis (Messer, 1994). Faces have these characteristics and infants are interested in faces. In this way, babies begin to use visual information to form expectations for interaction and to model their own expressions on those they see. Gradually, by six months, babies learn to track parent gaze and movement to figure out not only how humans move (Brand, Shallcross, Sabatos, & Massie, 2007), but also how they interact.

In addition to the distance receptors of audition and vision, infants receive information via taste, smell, and touch as well. Infants express their preferences for sweet over salty, bananas over ammonia, by means of facial expressions which will continue to be an important way to convey their likes and dislikes. And if breast-fed, babies recognize their own mother's breast odor (Cernoch & Porter, 1985). Touch is particularly sensitive in the newborn around the mouth, the palms of the hands, and soles of the feet (Humphrey, 1978). For many months, parents can only guess what their infants' desires are, but the guesses are well informed by facial expressions quite similar to adult humans' that signal pleasure, avoidance, disgust, and so forth. Nonverbal communication is how the infant interacts and will continue to serve well throughout life. But once verbal communication begins, nonverbal signals typically assume a supplemental role.

The First Year of Interaction

Judging from the review so far, it might seem the infant can barely interact, and merely passively receives. Not so. Certainly the new baby has a lot to learn about the world, but also has a lot to express and does so through the facial expressions mentioned above, and a myriad of vocal expressions, from crying to cooing to babbling to speech. Nonverbal expressions become more controlled and purposeful gestures, while vocalized sounds become more meaningful and eventually symbolic. For a parent, these expressions gradually become clearer signals of the infant's needs. And meanwhile, the parent uses infant signals to create opportunities for interaction. For example, when Rico sees his bottle he grunts and reaches, opening the conversational door for his father: "Are you hungry? Let's have some breakfast before we go to the park." Now, Rico did not intend to start a conversation, but his father did. The parent provides the **scaffold** for the infant to build meaningful ways to interact.

Infant Interaction Cues

Vocalizations begin early and grow in sophistication. Perhaps the first never-fail attention getter is cry. Cry calls the adult to the helpless newborn and can inform the parent of the infant's state. Most parents, regardless of culture, respond to infant cry intuitively with soothing behaviors such as cradling to the body, rocking, and walking. This **intuitive parenting** continues as the young child begins to coo; the parent then responds with eye contact and vocalization (Keller, Scholmerich, & Eible-Eibesfeldt, 1988). Cooing sounds are pretty much limited to vowel sounds such as "ah" and "ooh" or a nasal, "mmm." Once the baby can sit up unaided, at around 6 months, respiration is more stable and the articulators are more mature (the larynx descends, the mouth grows larger leaving space for the tongue to move, and the first teeth erupt). Thus the baby can better control breath, tongue, and lips enabling the articulation of sounds. All of that means that consonants ("d," "p," "b") may be added to vowels to form syllables (Langlois, Baken, & Wilder, 1980; Yingling, 1981). The sounds of repetitive babbling, such as "bababa" or "duhduhduh," which closely resemble adult speech sounds, seem to be preferred by parents because they "frame the infant as a potential conversational partner" (Bloom & Lo, 1990). Now the parent is rewarded with sounds similar to their own, and the baby has the raw material for meaningful words. Before we look at that development, let's look at other early communicative behaviors.

Nonvocal signals include eye contact and smiles. Newborns search for a face when they hear speech and withdraw gaze when overwhelmed with stimuli. But gaze quickly becomes an attachment behavior as infant focus improves and parents respond with eye contact. Parents will work hard to get a smile from a baby, but the rare newborn smile is more likely a response to some internal state (yes, such as "gas") than to interaction. But by 3 months infants smile more often to their parents than to unfamiliar people (Camras, Malatesta, & Izard, 1991) so the smile begins to be a social behavior. For a more complete list of communication developments in the first four years, see Table 2.1 at the end of this chapter.

Parent Interaction Factors

Bonding behavior between parents and children has been described in terms of **attachment** theory. Secure attachments are linked

24

to interactional synchrony – the smooth coordination of action between the two partners. However, many factors can affect the smoothness of their interaction, including the existing family system. Much of the attachment research has studied the mother–child link so we are not as certain about the father–child bond, although an instrument to measure fathers' attachment has been developed recently (Condon & Corkindale, 2008).

In 1991, Belsky and colleagues concluded that mother accounts for infant stability – less negative emotion with time – while the bond with father accounts for any increases in negative infant emotion. For example, a father who is uninvolved and dissatisfied with marriage will create a system dynamic in which mother responds by being over involved with her infant. They suggest that it is the family system that affects psychological health, marital satisfaction, and smooth maternal interaction with the infant (Belsky, Fish, & Isabella, 1991). A conflicted mother–father relationship is likely associated with mother's insensitivity and lack of responsiveness to her infant and attachment insecurity in the infant (Finger, Hans, Bernstein, & Cox, 2009). Undoubtedly, there are many factors affecting the family system: individual health, motivations for parenting, marriage relationship, and external stressors to name a few. In theory, the attachment style formed in first interactions leads the child to develop an "internal working model" that informs the child's expectations for not only mother's behavior but for later relationships. In later chapters, we will examine some of the reported effects. But this research raises a question about parental influence: Why is mother assumed to be the critical parent? What of "fatherese?"

Mothering and fathering. We know much more about mothers' influence than about fathers' and other caregivers' effects. Mothers have made themselves more available as research subjects, due to both the physiology of birthing and our cultural bias for mothers to provide early care. In any case, there is a lot of variation in mothers' speech styles. If her interaction focuses on referencing things (using words for objects and events), her baby a few months hence is more likely to specialize in those words (nouns). If her style is more expressive (lots of intonation or "music" in her tone of voice) her infant will emphasize early intonation (Dore, 1974). But children are not only soaking up what mothers give them. As infants mature, mothers gradually introduce conversational features to their speech. First they model turn-taking by responding vocally to the child's vocalizations and gestures. Then mothers use questions ("What do you want? Want the ball?") to cue an appropriate response until the baby is able to create a message ("Bauw!") without prompting (Moerk, 1974).

Fathers are often assumed to be less interested and less involved in nurturing infants. But, in one early study, fathers typically were as communicatively involved (touching, kissing, vocalizing) with newborns as mothers, but they fed infants less often than mothers did (Parke & Sawain, 1981). Are dads at the mercy of cultural expectations about who does the caretaking? Lamb (1987) found that mothers and fathers are equally competent, but that because mothers often spend more time in childcare, fathers come to feel less competent in reading the baby's needs. Recently, Combs-Orme and Renkert (2009) found two classes of fathering behavior for both residential and non-residential dads: those who displayed low levels of both caregiving and affection, and those who were high in both. So, biological fathers evidently have a choice about nurturing, and see caregiving and affection as a package deal. The only exception is the surrogate father (non-biological: stepfather, uncle, etc.) who is more likely to separate out the two behaviors and provide affection but little caregiving.

Regardless of how the differences arise, mothers hold babies to take care of them (feed, bathe, etc.) while fathers more often hold infants to play with them. Fathers are generally more physically playful with babies, while mothers are more verbally playful. Fathers also encourage more gender-stereotyped behaviors (Snow, Jacklin, & Maccoby, 1983). For example, father is more likely to offer his boy a ball or truck, whereas mother may be more tolerant of the baby's choice of a doll. Overall, fathers provide the scaffolding for physical play and culturally appropriate gender roles while mothers model verbal play and flexibility to individual needs and differences. But social class and culture also can affect how parents structure the social world.

Socioeconomic differences in parenting? Basil Bernstein (1971, 1973, 1977) suggested that speech differences among social classes could influence children's abilities to express themselves in a variety of situations. He identified two codes: elaborated and restricted. **Elaborated codes** – semantically abstract and syntactically complex – make for clear messages regardless of the listener or context (e.g. "Please be at ease. I will need several minutes to complete preparations.") **Restrictive codes** – semantically condensed and syntactically simple – rely more on nonverbal expressions and verbal shortcuts to share meanings between similar speakers ("Chill. Gimme one sec."). Clearly, we all use restricted code at certain times, with certain people. But if we were not also capable of using elaborated code, we would find ourselves unable to make sense to one from outside our social circle. Bernstein's research was performed in Great Britain, where social class distinctions have been more formal than in the US, although those distinctions have been blurred more recently (Grace, 2008).

Does the theory hold true elsewhere? Middle-class mothers tend to use elaborated code to control their children (Cook-Gumperz, 1973), but we might actually be looking at education rather than class as the important factor. Obviously, middle-class mothers often have more time for interaction than less advantaged moms who have, perhaps, less education and less free time. What we do know is that maternal reading seems to minimize class differences in mother–child interaction (Hoff-Ginsberg, 1991). Parents who have or make the time to read and converse with their children are more likely to adapt their speech for the language learner, while parents who feel time and money pressures may rely on the language shortcuts available in restricted code.

Cultural variations in parenting. Some parenting behaviors are intuitive, such as rocking to soothe, stressing meaningful features of speech (ACL), and engaging with infant in object play (with a toy, often). What varies across cultures is *how* the parent talks about the play. For example, European mothers use talk to *describe* the play – they frame what they are doing and the properties of the toy with speech (e.g. "Here's a red, round ball. Now push it back to Mommy.") In contrast, African mothers emphasize *social* relationships rather than objects ("Your Mama is here to get that for you.") (Rabain-Jamin, 1989).

Mothers also vary in their responsiveness to infant attention-getting behavior. Kenyan mothers respond physically, such as holding the baby, while US and Mexican mothers reacted to infant cry, gaze or vocalization with more talking and looking to the child (Richman, Miller, & LeVine, 1992). To complicate matters a bit, the higher the educational level, the more talking was used rather than simple eye contact. So, again, education may be the factor of interest rather than culture.

But aside from word choice, basic ACL seems similar across cultures. Among German, English, and Mandarin Chinese, ACL features were consistent – longer pauses, shorter phrases, higher pitch, and longer intonation contours – despite very different languages and word preferences (Grieser & Kuhl, 1988).

Beyond the use of ACL to mark speech features, mothers choose particular kinds of words to spread cultural values. Comparing US and Japanese mothers, Toda, Fogel, and Kawai (1990) found American moms used more imperatives (directions) and yes–no questions, while Japanese moms typically spoke to their babies with variations of nonsense sounds. They conclude that in Japan, the interaction goals are to empathize with the infant (sound like the infant) and acknowledge distinctively baby-like qualities, whereas in the US, the goals are to express authority and encourage individual expression. Later in the child's first year, many mothers across cultures increase informative speech to match the baby's increased interest in objects. Nonetheless, Japanese mothers who prefer an empathic style still used more affective speech (emotionally expressive), while Argentinian mothers who favor an authoritative style used more direct statements (Borstein, Tal, & Rahn, 1992). The goal of mothers globally is to acculturate their babies, so the way language skills are introduced naturally varies to accommodate that goal.

Individual differences in parenting. In addition to the gender variations we noted in mothering and fathering, parents assume a range of parenting styles, probably depending upon the styles their own parents used and whether they wish to emulate or distinguish themselves from the familiar style. In terms of the style with which parents exert control, Baumrind (1968) found three clusters of behaviors: **authoritarian** (demanding, unresponsive, and adult-centered), **authoritative** (encouraging, reasoned, and child-centered), or **permissive** (nondirective and disorganized). Bayer and Cegala (1992) found the first two styles to be related to communication style: **verbal aggressiveness** is related to authoritarian parenting (unilateral messages) while **argumentativeness** is related to authoritative parenting (verbal give-and-take). The first, my-way-or-the-highway style affects the child's self-concept negatively, while the second let's-talk-about-it style does not. Because these communication styles seem to be relatively stable (Infante & Rancer, 1982), such predispositions could be identified in parenting programs before an authoritarian style becomes the default parenting mode. Infante and his colleagues (Infante, Chandler, & Rudd, 1989) have found success in training verbally aggressive spouses to use more argumentative communication, so it is likely the same would hold true for parents who wish to avoid verbal aggression with children.

A recent study linked parental verbal aggression to insecure child attachment. Adult children (college students) with a secure attachment style perceived their parents as higher in responsiveness and lower in verbal aggression than children with nonsecure attachment styles (Roberto, Carlyle, Goodall, & Castle, 2009). So, parenting style has long-term effects on children's later capacities for enduring relationships.

Parents and children arrive at their relationship with very different agendas and wildly varying skill sets. But one goal they share: to establish and maintain a relationship, and that is what holds them together despite their differences.

Communication, Language, and Media: Learning the Ropes

Once all the necessary components are in place – infant sensory abilities and social predispositions, parent skill and willingness to engage – the process of development builds momentum, adding meanings to build a mind, and engaging media to broaden experience beyond the immediate.

Learning to Speak: Gestures to Symbols

The infant's gradual acquisition of symbols is a move from simple gestures and vocalizations to meaningful sounds to fully symbolic words. Reaching becomes pointing; sounds become words; words are combined syntactically to form sentences. This build-up of meaning occurs over about a two-year period.

Early conversations between parent and child are orchestrated by the parent but reciprocated by the child. When a parent plays "peekaboo," the baby is looking for the pattern in the interaction. When it is repeated, the child comes to anticipate the parent's sequence: (1) parent saying baby's name ("Benny!"), (2) covering her eyes and repeating the name call several times, and finally (3) simultaneously uncovering the eyes with the cry "Peekaboo!" Having practiced this before, 5-month-old Benny begins to wriggle his body in anticipation during steps 1 and 2, but keep his eyes wide open. At the step 3, he giggles, smiles, and releases his body tension. These first **scripts** are learned in highly structured contexts directed by the adult. Gradually, infants learn scripts and then adapt them when there's a discrepancy between the original script and the new situation. Indeed, baby may change the script himself. At 7 months, Benny has learned the game of take-and-give. First, he learned the "take" portion by grasping what was offered (a mirrored rattle). Slowly, he learned that his mother's expectation was that he should "give" it back to her. In one interaction Julie observed (Yingling, 1990/91), "Benny," having been particularly intrigued by a mirrored rattle that was new to him, cooperated through a few turns of take-and-give with mother. Then he twisted away from her, clearly not wanting to give her the toy. As she persisted, saying: "Give Momma the toy," he drew back the rattle and hit her on the arm with it. Mother reacted with, "Does that mean 'No'?" Well, probably, as she let him keep the toy! Over a period of several months, he had learned his own part in controlling the interaction. This sort of educational play relies on the abilities of both parties to interact about a joint referent.

Joint referencing occurs before symbol use, so uses gesture as well as sound to stand for things. This is done in dialogue; it is a process of developing procedures for constructing meaning together. Bruner (1977) identified three aspects of early referencing: (1) **indicating** or using communication cues to bring the partner's attention to something, (2) **deixis** or using features of the context to aid in joint referencing, and (3) **predication** or using symbols to name the events or things of interest.

Early indicating occurs when a parent tracks his baby's gaze to see what is interesting to her. On her side, the infant learns to track the parent's line of regard as early as 4 months (Scaife & Bruner, 1975). Deixis comes a bit later when the older baby marks the target of interest by pointing or touching. However, much earlier, the infant may reach for something and the parent, recognizing the gesture, treats it as pointing. Thus the infant comes to rely on the reaching gesture to indicate interest and it turns into a gesture meaning roughly: "that is of interest to me" which is quite a different gesture from the simple reach as an attempt to grasp something. Predication is only possible once symbolizing begins, around 18 months. Then the child can comment upon the object of interest. So, for example, as long as the object is in sight, the child need not name it, as the name gives no more information than the pointing gesture. So, instead, the child points to the ball, saying "Gimme!" or points to Dad's car, saying "Go!" Even though the meaning is still limited ("Who goes? Dad, baby, both?"), predication gives much more information than indicating or deixis alone. It says something about the interesting object to a willing partner.

Turn-taking is a basic requirement of symbolic interaction. When communication is spoken, one must speak as the other listens or all we have left are dueling monologues. We've all had them, but they are not the dialogues that make for co-creating meaning. Fortunately, babies are very interested in what adults have to say, as they pay attention to the sound patterns to detect something familiar or predictable. By 3 or 4 months of age, parents and babies use two patterns of interaction: co-action in which the partners vocalize simultaneously and a turn-like pattern in which partners alternate vocalizations between them (Stern, Jaffe, Beebe, & Bennett, 1975). Neither pattern disappears entirely. We vocalize together when we moan, shout, cry, cheer, hoot, and howl; when our feelings are aroused in the same way. But when we really want to hear others, learn who they are or what they know, we give up the conversational floor to hear them. These kinds of turn patterns require self-regulation as well as the desire to know. When we can control our own strong feelings in favor of cognitive activity, we can stop speaking and hear.

From 6 to 9 months, infants gradually produce longer runs of vocalizations while parents shorten their own turns (Yingling, 1984). At first, it is up to the adult to demonstrate language, but as the child is able to articulate longer runs of syllables, the willing parent will give up the conversational floor to demonstrate the cooperative nature of communication.

Protosymbols are possible as soon as the child begins the sequence to categorize, differentiate, and generalize meaning. Recall from Chapter 1 that categorizing and differentiating are characteristics of representation. Now we'll examine how the child builds meaning. Categorizing is a process of grouping several qualities to one signal. Julie's niece, Sam, late in her first year, uttered her first recognizable word: "goggie." Never mind that her mother was dismayed that it was not "Mommie," Sam had discovered a sound to represent the interesting creature that lived next door. She could not point to him when he wasn't there, as he most of the time was not, so she *needed* the sound. At first, "goggie" was just the mutt next door, but pretty soon Sam realized she wanted to talk about lots of living creatures but she still had just this one word. Then generalization came in handy. Once she had a useful sound that others understood, she could use it to talk about any interesting animal. Indeed, another baby of Julie's acquaintance learned "duck" to talk about the animals in his yard and then used it to refer to all the domestic animals as well as his father. Much as these developments may be temporarily disturbing to parents (well, these parents anyway), they pave the way for differentiation and thus contrast.

Once differentiation begins, then finer categories are possible. Sam learns that not all animals are dogs, but all dogs are animals. A dog is not a cat is not an elephant and so on. This capacity to imply what something is as well as what it is not is the hallmark of symbolism. Without some notion of what a dog is *not*, we would have no solid concept of dog. This building of meaning on the basis of contrast is what Kelly (1969/1979) called a **construct**. What is involved is not merely constructing two poles of meaning within a larger category system of living beings – dog and not-dog (e.g. fish, toad, snake, etc.) – but realizing also that neither pole of the dogness construct has anything to do with a boot. The poles may be similar in their applicability to living, moving things and yet qualitatively different (furry and four-legged vs. scaly and finned). Once the child is able to consider several categories of thought at once in this way, analytic thought becomes possible. Before we turn to higher-order thought processes, we will look at how these symbolic processes eventually can be performed silently.

Speaking to Learn: Egocentric to Inner to Socialized Speech

The young child speaks egocentrically in order to figure out difficult problems with words. When thoughts are spoken to solve problems that have not yet been internalized, we observe **private** speech. Preschoolers who use more private speech are more likely to complete tasks independently than those who used less private speech (Chiu & Alexander, 2000).

But speech for oneself continues to be useful throughout life, to daydream, rehearse, imagine. You may have had the experience of speaking aloud for your own purposes. A student of Julie's gave the example of her first day on the job as a lifeguard. She was trained in all the techniques, but had never been called upon to use them in a real emergency. As she sat on her chair, she heard the first shouts for help. And found that she was saying out loud: "Grab the float; whistle for assistance; get out there!" She was running through the procedures but needed the structure of words to regulate her actions. This is observable, audible thought.

Private speech and **inner speech** serve similar purposes but take

33

different forms. Private speech is voluntary and vocalized. Inner speech is also voluntary and self-directed, but is covert, silent. In the toddler, the problem-solving that private speech affords is absorbed into a process called mind and becomes inner speech that serves thought. Wertsch (1979) explained that inner speech has a specialized structure that we can often observe in egocentric and private speech before they are internalized: abbreviation and predication. Abbreviation in this case means that many of the syntactical structures used to help others understand us are omitted (subject of the sentence, articles, and other modifiers). Predication is "the basic syntactic form of inner speech (pp. 287–288), meaning that the action is the important information for self whereas the topic is understood. For example, notice that in our example above, the notable words are "grab," "whistle," and "get." You might observe that children feature predicates when they begin to speak and continue to rely on them as they tell themselves how to solve problems. So, as inner speech proceeds, what becomes of external speech?

As speech is internalized, toddlers' spoken words become more informed by their inner speech. The child who approaches 7 years appears more and more to be "thinking before speaking" and indeed is doing just that. Their sentences are fully formed and grammatical so another can grasp their meaning. This socialized speech is served by the increasing abilities of the child to imagine what the other person is feeling and how they are motivated.

Learning about Others: Empathy to Role Play to Perspective Taking

Very young children have **empathy** for others; they recognize reactions to feelings as being similar to their own and they often want to help the other to "feel better" when they perceive the signs of distress. Toddlers use words like "happy" and "sad" at around 2 years (Smiley & Huttenlocher, 1989), first for their own feelings, then for others'. By 2½ years, they begin to infer others' internal states.

Later, in their eagerness to learn what it is like to be a mom, or a salesperson, or a teacher, children try on those roles and approximate the behaviors they observe. In that way, they not only check out behaviors for their own identities, but they practice "walking a mile in the other's shoes" thereby imagining the other's motivations and choices from that position. At the Children's Museum in Boston, Julie observed this interchange in the "grocery store" setting within. The most popular position is at the cash register and Olivia had waited for her turn. As she pulled her "customer's" selections toward her, she named each item and called out the price: "Bread: $3.50!" Her "customer" broke in at this point with "Isn't that a lot?" Olivia replied: "Well, do you want it or don't you?" Olivia has clearly observed cashiers and customers, is practicing what she would say in that position, what her motivation would be, and how it feels to be in that role.

Over the course of many interactions, Olivia observes how people behave, guesses how they might feel, and in **role play**, she gets to try on different positions and clarify who she is in relation to others. Additionally, she begins to learn what motivates others so she can ultimately put herself in another's position, cognitively, and use that knowledge to adjust her speech with them. This **perspective-taking** ability is not possible until inner speech serves socialized speech.

Internalizing for Thought: Memory, Scripts, Problem-solving

Once the child has internalized the ability to solve problems, then all manner of cognitive abilities are potential. First, the use of symbols for voluntary recall serves to stretch memory. Then **scripts** are built from that ability to remember commonly used routines of appropriate and successful communication behaviors in various settings. Recognition memory is the earliest kind available and those memories return to us unbidden. When a set of associations (mother's love at Christmas) is linked to a stimulus (the smell of sugar cookies baking) the memory is stored in neural networks to be involuntarily cued when that aromatic stimulus arises again. However, voluntary or free recall relies on cues we can control, either internalized words we can use for covert recall, or external props such as knots in rope for counting days.

Very young children rely first on others to aid their voluntary memory. For example, when Ned's mother is running late and tells Ned to find his mittens, she probably is not too surprised when he can't find them. So, she provides prompts: "Where were you when you last had them on? Out in the yard?" And off Ned runs to find them next to the snowman. Later, when children can use symbols to hold an idea, their memory improves. Toward the end of the second year, they are able to hold two items in memory and establish a relationship between them (Hartup, 1985, p. 69). This is not only the beginning of simple logical chains (if A, then B; or "if snowman, then mittens") but also the sequence of events that form scripts. Recall that infants do learn scripts as a recognizable pattern but probably cannot break down the pattern for analysis or variation. Later, Ned's toddler script for "going shopping with Dad" probably has many variations that allow for freedom at choice points (e.g. as we enter a store, I can choose to ride in the cart, or walk beside it, or help push it). Over the course of many cycles of interaction sequences, Ned internalizes sets of possible sequences for each script and thus increases his adaptability to interaction.

Vygotsky pointed out that memory is the earliest stage of cognitive development which then serves more complex forms of thought: "For the young child, to think means to recall; but for the adolescent, to recall means to think" (1978, pp. 50–51). Gradually problem-solving goes beyond the simple causal reasoning of "if A, then B" to more complex analytic chains which are often learned, again, by working with others to reason out problems. Forman and Cazden (1985) set up problem-solving sessions with middle-school students working on chemistry experiments. They found three kinds of interactions: parallel (sharing materials but little monitoring of others' work or sharing one's own), associative (exchanging information but no coordination), and cooperative (constant monitoring of others' work and coordinating roles). Overall, pairs of students solved problems faster than singletons. But the one pair who discovered cooperative interaction first solved more problems than other pairs. Children learn analytic skills by interacting with others. Parents are usually a child's most cognitively mature interactants, and as such they greatly influence the child's growing cognitive skills.

Pragmatics: Strategies, and Skills to Communicate

The **pragmatics** of communication refers to the necessary strategies and skills for getting commonplace things done. Daily, we accomplish the exchange of goods and services, the construction and maintenance of relationships, the judicial use of control in home and work, and so forth. These are all pragmatic accomplishments of interaction. We will look at several practical interaction accomplishments that require strategy and skill: conflict and persuasion, disclosure and deception, support and comfort.

Conflict inevitably occurs in parent–child interaction when the child has a point of view to call her own, and it does not jibe with the parental view. Despite how these conflicts may feel as they first arise, parents can take comfort from the knowledge that practice with conflict fosters the development of perspective-taking (Selman, 1980). So, these early conflicts are not only necessary, but also developmental. Mother–child conflicts begin simply (often with the child's early negation ("No!") at 18 months or so, though they can occur nonverbally with a younger child who, say, refuses to give up a toy. Older children successfully use coercion (ignoring or disapproving) to get what they want about half of the time; and punishment of that tactic increases the child's use of it (Patterson, 1979)! So parents, beware of punishing a child's conflict behavior. When a child has few strategies to get what they want, they are likely to persist in that strategy whether it works or not. Rather than reinforce unwanted behavior, parents would do better to model and encourage new skills. (We discuss conflict at greater length in Chapter 4, where Tom shares his parenting technique of asking for three reasons.)

Persuasion involves the use of symbols to attempt to influence another's thoughts or behaviors, and stands in contrast to coercion, which is the use of force, physical or psychological, to influence another. Because persuasion requires both verbal skill and the ability to appeal to the target's interests, it is not only a learned set of skills, but requires strategies that rely on perspective-taking. Indeed, the older the child, the more sophisticated the appeals. Haslett (1983) noted a shift at age 3 when children are still using reactive strategies (denials based on prior messages, e.g. "No, you can't [do what you just said you'd do]") but are beginning to use assertions, counter-assertions, and questions (p. 94). By 4 years, they use more active strategies (independent of prior messages) and can use several in support of one position. And, they are starting to personalize their strategies for the needs of a particular other. When a child can use one strategy on Dad (e.g. "I'll help wash your car if you take me to the playground") and another on Mom (e.g. "I'll eat my vegetables tonight if I can have ice cream now") then that child likely is taking the perspective of his targets to persuade. This is a child who probably has engaged in conflict interactions, and the practice is paying off. Gradually the persuasive skills will mature until – especially if the parenting is authoritative – the teenager can engage in reasoned argument. Such a teen will be more likely to rely on his verbal skill than the loudness of his insults or the strength of his fists.

Disclosure and deception are flip sides of expressivity. The former is the revelation of some perceived truth about oneself, while the latter is the withholding of information. Parents typically believe that the first is a sign of a good relationship with their children, while the second must indicate some trouble or failure between them. But these two ways of presenting self must both be practiced by every child who is still learning who that self is and is to be. Dindia (1998) described the two poles of self-presentation as "the dialectical contradiction between the need to reveal and the need to conceal" (p. 104). As the child constructs a self, she tries on roles that she knows are removed from what is "real." Role play and imaginative play are forays into what-might-be, as are versions of the self the child tries on and adjusts. The self is such a fluid concept in childhood that, even while they need to express themselves, they also need to protect their budding identities against the judgments others can make of those who are less skilled. It makes sense that children who need to protect their boundaries the most – those who are judged most harshly – will improve their deception skills the most.

Early attachment experience may affect the balance a child finds between disclosure and deception (Hazen & Shaver, 1987). Secure individuals who had parents sensitive to their needs reported that they found it easy to disclose and get close to others. Those who developed avoidant attachment styles had parents who were insensitive to their needs and were uncomfortable in revealing themselves. Anxious/ambivalent types whose parents were inconsistent in meeting their needs saw relationships as a struggle between intimacy and loss; they worried about the effects of their disclosures. Thus, the way that parents meet their infants' needs may affect their later capacities to sustain and enjoy intimate relationships.

In very difficult circumstances, children are challenged to form rules for disclosing (or not) damaging information. Petronio, Reeder, Hecht, and Ros-Mendoza (1996) called these "boundary access rules" that children and teens use to reveal information (in their study, about sexual abuse) and "boundary protection rules" to preserve privacy. Access rules involved choosing safe places to disclose, building the degree of disclosure, and obtaining the permission of the listener to hear the disclosure. Protection rules limit disclosure by assessing listeners' responsiveness, trustworthiness, ability to understand, and possible reactions to the information.

Consider this example that Julie experienced with the 16-year-old sister of an intimate friend. Stephanie, we'll call her, was visiting her oldest brother from her parents' home a thousand miles away. Julie offered to take her to breakfast at a restaurant where she met a female study-pal every Saturday. As they ate, Stephanie listened to the conversation between good friends, and allowed herself to be drawn in by questions from the older women. She gradually gave information about herself, which was accepted, until she revealed that she was seeing a therapist because she had moved ahead of her peers to early college work. A few more disclosures and Stephanie revealed that her middle brother (whom Julie had never met) had been abusing her for years. Fighting for composure and calm, Julie asked if she'd revealed this to anyone else. Stephanie had not. Julie managed to get a commitment from Stephanie that she would tell her therapist. Ultimately, she told her older brother and parents as well. Consider Stephanie's situation: she realized her family dynamic would be damaged by this news and did not want to be the cause, Julie seemed trustworthy and responsive, and the restaurant was a safe spot where no one would make a scene. Stephanie built her disclosure gradually and received tacit permission to tell what could be most damaging to her family and her self-concept. The balance of disclosure and deception rides a teetering, changing self-concept for many years. The best parents can do is to maximize their trustworthiness and responsiveness, and perhaps to encourage safe relationships with other trustworthy adults who are not so entrenched in the family network as to make some disclosures nearly impossible.

One final note about disclosure concerns digital communication. Many children (middle school through teens) find it easier to share personal information via their computer or cell phone (and thus, with perfect strangers as well as friends) than in a face-to-face interaction with a possibly disapproving adult. Although such a choice may not be well informed or even safe, it is understandable. On one hand, such personal expression helps develop personal identity; on the other, it helps support her social identity as a group member. The paradox that Palfrey and Gasser (2008) note is that a teen may create multiple identities with ease, thus appearing to have more control over identity, but indeed has much less control than teens in earlier eras (p. 34). Reinvention may still be dream, but has become harder to actualize.

Support and comfort are similar sets of positive behaviors that rest upon complex social knowledge, including empathy and perspective-taking. Supportive communication includes communication sensitivity and comforting acts.

A sensitive conversationalist has a good memory for conversation, detects meanings accurately, is interested in listening, and can come up with a variety of ways of saying something (Daly, Vangelisti, & Daughton, 1987). This is a conversationalist who can monitor his own behavior and figure out his partner's communication needs. This is a sophisticated set of behaviors for parents to model but will take a long time to master. However, comforting behavior can start young.

Comforting messages are intended to lessen the emotional distress of others and convey "care, commitment, and interest" (Burleson, 1994, p. 5). Parents are the primary source of intimacy, material assistance, affection, and reassurance of the child's worth (Furman & Buhrmester, 1985). And, children of supportive parents have many advantages: better mental and physical health, higher self-esteem, and fewer behavioral problems, less depression and unhappiness, better peer relationships and better school performance (Gardner & Cutrona, 2004). Comforting parents have comforting children. Mothers who used sophisticated comforting strategies (listener centered, feeling centered, accepting of partner) had children who were more advanced in social-cognitive development than children of less comforting mothers (Applegate, Burleson, & Delia, 1992). Once the model of comforting is structured between parent and child and practiced, then comforting becomes the norm in that system. The adage, "The apple never falls far from the tree," refers to more than genetic similarities; it is about the long-term effects of communication scaffolding.

Parents typically have great influence on their children's spoken language skills. Lately it seems that many parents have thrown up their hands in dismay over their lack of influence when it comes to other media effects. Is it really hopeless?

Spoken Language to Written Language

Media are simply the means of transmission we use to communicate. Spoken communication uses airwaves as a channel; written communication is a visual mode using light. Unfortunately, the term "media" has been adopted to mean only electronic media and that can be misleading. The medium we use makes a difference to how we make sense of our world. Or, as Marshall McLuhan (1962) famously said, the medium *is* the message. Moreover, the order in which media are acquired can make a very big difference to developing individuals and to their accompanying sense-making constructions.

For quite a long time, spoken language was all we had aside from nonverbal gestures and expressions. Then some very bright person or tribe figured out that sound could be represented visually, and the alphabet was created. That alone caused a huge upheaval in human sense making (Ong, 1967, 1982) including power differentials between those who controlled information and those who did not. The spread of literacy and print democratized information again, but also made possible the private sense of individuality to which we've become accustomed. Consider similar effects on the child.

The process of learning to read and write is more complex than you might now recall, from your position of long literacy. But it is a hard-won skill. For writing, children must develop motor skill and that takes time. By 4 years, the child usually has drawn their first picture of a person, and by 6 years, they can copy some numbers and simple words (Berk, 1998, p. 217). But even before that, preschoolers understand quite a lot about written language, especially if they are immersed in a literate family. The first development is metalinguistic awareness, or the recognition that those marks on paper or billboard or computer screen are meaningful. Families that stock print material – magazines, newspapers, books – can have children who develop metalinguistic awareness as early as 3 (Chaney, 1994). Gradually, children learn some characteristics of print language (e.g. stories are written left to right; shopping lists in a column), and then begin to analyze how letters and sounds are linked systematically and begin to invent spellings between 5 and 7 years. Once they switch to standard spellings and begin to study formal grammar in school, children are well on their way to experiencing the private world of reading and the power that accompanies writing. Writing and reading tend to isolate and individualize us; electronic media tend to globalize and link us (see Ong, 1967, 1982). Considering the fact that toddlers are being introduced to computers, how might learning print and digital literacy at the same time affect the developing mind?

Electronic Media: Ubiquitous, Interactive, and Transformative

What happens when children use a computer before they learn to write? Or even before they speak? These are not trivial questions; the first is at issue now, the second has been proposed and will surely happen.

As you know, children learn to communicate by using the inter-action framework, or scaffold, that adults have built for them. Apparently, as long as adults continue to scaffold media use, then media may be employed usefully to good effect. However, many a parent is not computer savvy and some may not even own a computer. What then?

The child guided or not, has many options via the computer: games, educational programs, audiobooks, and so forth. The use of educational software is more likely if parents use it, or are at least aware of educational applications. However, gaming has become the most common use of computers for children aged 2–18 (Roberts, Foehr, Rideout, & Brodie, 1999) and that is problematic as games come in many guises. Our concerns about violence on television pale in comparison to an interactive environment that rewards aggressive behavior with points, access to new levels and so forth.

Right through the teenage years, the prefrontal cortex is not fully functioning to analyze and evaluate risks and consequences, so children fail to recognize what effects might accrue to aggressive behavior or ill-considered self-portrayals online (Palfrey & Gasser, 2008, p. 166). For example, when a child chooses to "play" a character with specific strengths, as in *Mortal Kombat* or *World of Warcraft,* the scene is set for role play in which a violent persona is practiced (Dill & Dill, 1998). Children are attracted to high levels of action and explosive effects, and without any restrictions, will play whatever games give them the desired excitement. But, parents and teachers have to understand this attraction and be willing to set limits, especially for young children, on gaming and exposure to violent activities (Palfrey & Gasser, 2008, p. 221).

Alternatives to games may not be as thrilling but certainly more likely to initiate creativity and thinking skills. Programs such as

StoryMat allow the child to collaborate by telling a story which is recorded on the "mat" and then similar stories are played back to stimulate the child's further storytelling. This sort of activity provides a bridge to written literacy (Cassell & Ryokai, 2001). Children are using computers at the age of 3 or even before. And that can be handled well or poorly. A loving parent can introduce a 3-year-old to computers because he knows what the child is ready for and can then allow the child to take ownership of the learning process (Lacina, 2007). As they can provide a jump to print literacy, story programs and book sites are a good start (examples from Lacina, 2007, include: KidSpace@the Internet, The International Children's Library, and StoryLine Online).

So the question is not whether the medium is good or bad inherently, but whether caregivers are present to scaffold the experience. Media do have effects, in and of themselves, but parental effects in concert with media will be critical in terms of how the child learns to use them. As children learn to read by way of literacy in the home (e.g. bedtime stories, reading instructions, labels, etc.), so children learn television literacy by watching shows and talking about them with adults and older siblings, and further, learn to handle digital media in interaction with more sophisticated others as well. But, many of the "born digital" generation have learned to perform online identities in the company of peers rather than trusted adults. These self-presentations via MySpace, Facebook, or other social network sites establish group memberships, but also send personal information to unknown entities with unknown results, nearly infinite shelf-life, and loss of control over the information (Palfrey & Gasser, 2008). The effects on what should be a still flexible identity can be deep and damaging. Parents will have to be very observant of a child's changing behavior to detect spiraling self-esteem. Far preferable would be participation in the child's online activity, but is it likely?

In 1990, Kubey and Csikszentmihalyi proposed that television viewing is at its best as a family pastime. People do other things while they are watching TV, and talking is one of the best things to do with children in the room. But digital communication is largely a silent activity. Long before electronic anything, Plato claimed "a sound education consists in training people to find pleasure and pain in the right objects" (p. 214). Kubey & Csikszentmihalyi suggest that parents are key to developing competency (appropriate "pleasure and pain") in media literacy.

However, this is getting harder and harder for parents to do. Media convergence is a process by which "formerly distinct methods of communication merge to create new media" (Wartella, O'Keefe, & Scantlin, 2000). Take for example the emergence of electronic mail from the computer innovation of the Internet. Believe it or not, that was a relatively recent creation, but then it moved from e-mail to IM, then jumped to SMS (texting) and tweeting via cell phones. Few parents become familiar with new digital media before their teens do. So, the best that parents can do is to scaffold when they can by interacting with the media along with their children. Many a parent has joined Facebook and used Twitter to interact on the fly with children. And when all else fails, a willing uncle or aunt or family friend may be the family technology guru. The bottom line is to keep involved with children, no matter where their media take them.

Media transform. We certainly are different people in a literate culture than a preliterate one. And, McLuhan and Ong would attest, we are different people in a digital culture than in only a literate one. McLuhan forecast the "global village" that we are fast becoming. Providing more detail, Birkerts proposed (1994) that the gains of the electronic age include: a more global perspective, expanded neural capacity, a relativistic understanding of situations, and a readiness to try new arrangements. All well and good, but on the other hand, he also said we are losing: a fragmented sense of time such as experienced in reverie, a shattered faith in institutions and the narratives that shape subjective experience, a divorce from the past, an estrangement from geographic place, and an absence of any "strong vision of a personal or collective future" (p. 27). Time will tell, but consider the possibilities and what the effects of such losses would be.

Many older adults who watched the TV set enter the house in the 1950s are left gasping at the level of "interactivity" that young people experience. But is that electronic interactivity taking the place of more intimate face-to-face interaction? Will we lose the capacity for deep and close interaction? We don't know. But stay tuned and keep talking – especially to children. We will explore better ways to use media in Chapter 6.

In the next chapter, we examine family units and family relationships, including family leadership, sibling relationships, the further development of social skills, and communication to manage intimacy.

Table 2.1 Children's Nonverbal and Verbal Communication: Ages 0–4*

Age	What to expect:
Birth – 3 months	Nonverbal:
	Face: Tongue movements, gastric smiles, social smile (6–8 weeks)
	Eyes: Unfocused images, double vision, images noticed at 8 inches or closer
	Body: Erratic movement (until about 3 months).
	Gesture: Coordinated with sound production (@ 2–3 months)
	Space: Interaction in intimate proxemic zone
	Verbal:
	Receiving: General ability to discriminate vocal tones, including speech syllables, recognition of voices
	Sending: Distress cries, cries in five tones
3 – 6 months	Nonverbal:
	Face: Social smiles, distress/excitement/delight expressions (3 months)
	Eyes: Increasing ability to focus and see whole faces, follows other's gaze (beginning of indicating)
	Body: Increasing controlled movements
	Gesture: Parallels sound production, control may increase
	Space: Interaction in intimate proxemic zone

Table 2.1   *(continued)*

Age	What to expect:
	Verbal:
	Receiving: Increasing ability to discriminate vocal tones, recognition of voices, can begin to detect pauses, Sending: Cooing, beginning of babbling; re-vocalization of others' sounds; pre-verbal communication routines
6 – 12 months	Nonverbal:
	Face: Responsive smiling, begins to make faces, turns head Eyes: Able to focus, gaze, and follow images beyond 8 inches Body: Control increases of body Gesture: Reaching and hand use increasing control towards pointing, beginning of deixis (12–14 months) Space: Interaction continues in intimate proxemic zone
	Verbal:
	Receiving: Increasing ability to discriminate vocal tones, recognition of voices, can detect pauses, reacts to abrupt sound/visual changes
	Sending: Babbling repetitive syllables (6+ months), goo-ing (9+ months); speaks first word (high frequency sounds either referential (da da) or expressive (hi) (9–12+ months)); can begin to use messages to accomplish simple goals (getting an out-of-reach toy)
12 – 18 months	Nonverbal:
	Gesture: Pointing (12–14 months), point and gaze in different direction (14 months); begins poking, contact gestures Face: Increasing ability to portray emotions (fear, disgust, anger, distress, excitement) Space: Intimate proxemic zone continues and interaction in personal zone is added

Table 2.1 *(continued)*

Age	What to expect:
	Verbal:
	Linguistic communication increases, uses idiomorphs (sounds referring to an object or action: e.g., predication (symbols for action)), names for familiar others; new words added rapidly
18 months – 2 years	Nonverbal
	Control of body, gestures, and face increases; interaction continues in intimate and personal proxemic zones and social zone is added
	Verbal:
	Phonemic: [p, m, n, h, w, b; t, k, g, d, ng] Semantic: expressive children (more social/relational terms) referential children (more nouns); rapid vocabulary expansion Syntactic: single word utterances moving to two-words Pragmatic: increasing ability with speech acts like asking, naming, asserting, and more; turn-taking ability increases
2 – 4 years	Nonverbal:
	Nonverbal interaction becomes increasingly adult-like; widen proxemic zones to include social proxemic zone and public proxemic zone; gestures lessen in place of verbal cues
	Verbal:
	Learning to use egocentric speech; differences between referential and expressive children disappears; vocabulary expansion rapidly continues; conversational skills increase with use of longer utterances (3–5 words); participates in routine interactions, increases functional mastery of speech acts; expression of politeness conventions, early monitoring of own speech (monitoring increases at age 5)

* General profiles were compiled from information in Haslett and Samter (1997) and Wood (1981).

Activities

1. Discuss the implications of the finding that fathers encourage more gender-stereotyped behaviors in their children. Can you remember examples of this kind of childrearing from your childhood? How did it affect you?
2. What are the implications of cultural parenting differences, such as American parents using more descriptive and direc-tive speech, and Japanese and African parents using more empathic, emotive communication?
3. Consider the last time you experienced a failure of turn-taking (dueling monologues). What were the conditions of the interaction? How did you (or could you) repair it?
4. Think of a recent example of using private speech. Could you have solved the problem or completed the task without it? How? Would it have been more difficult? Easier? Would the result have taken longer, or been as successful?
5. Did you experience computers before you experienced print? Do you know anyone who did? With what effect?
6. Do you think computers will replace print entirely, as Birkerts fears? Do you think his fears about loss are warranted? If not, why not?

Suggested Further Reading

Birkerts, S. (1994). *The Gutenberg elegies.* NY: Fawcett Columbine.

Kubey, R., & Csikszentmihalyi, M. (1990). *Television and the quality of life: How viewing shapes everyday experience.* Hillsdale, NJ: Lawrence Erlbaum Associates.

Palfrey, J. & Gasser, U. (2008). *Born digital: Understanding the first generation of digital alternatives.* New York: Basic Books.

3

Children's Communication in Family Groups and Family Relationships

Nearly universally, we are born into groups of people who have already established relationships. And, because these units are **socially constructed** (i.e. are built using symbols and agreements about their meanings), children encounter incredible variety and richness as they experience relational and group communication processes at home. First, we look at the qualities of communication that children encounter in various types of families: nuclear, single-parent (residential, bi-residential), custodial grandparent, blended and stepfamilies, same-sex parented families, and polygamous families, as well as some of the relational communication processes in family units. Then we'll look at the various kinds of family relationships children may establish, starting with the primary caregivers, to siblings, and extended family members. Further, we'll see how those relationships ebb and flow by means of the push/pull **dialectics** found in all relationships. Finally, we'll suggest ways to promote positive communication development in family units and family relationships.

Types of Families

Humans are a creative and adaptive species, so there are potentially as many kinds of family configurations as there are constellations. Nevertheless, some family groupings seem to appear in certain parts of the world, as well as in particular historical periods, and cultural contexts. It is commonly believed for example, that **nuclear families** – mom, dad, and children – are a kind of default type of family unit, but that was not always the case, nor is it truly the case today. At certain points in history, extended families or tribes actually offered more protection and security and were more the norm. Polygamy, for example, has had a continued historical presence in the pantheon of family configurations. Let's take a brief tour of these various family types.

The nuclear family has been the cultural focus for childrearing in much of the world for the past century or so. In the US the nuclear family (biological parents and their offspring) is a legally protected entity, and that protection affords parents the freedom "to direct the upbringing and education of children" (*Meyer* v. *State of Nebraska*, 1925, p. 399). Because much of the research in the following sections is based on the nuclear family, and because other units may not be afforded the same attention or legal protection, we begin by reviewing alternative family configurations.

Single-Parent Families

The last century saw the glorification of the nuclear family as an ideal, but it also saw the erosion of its actual ability to maintain over time. By 2007, 39.7% of children born in the US were to unmarried mothers (Hamilton, Martin, & Ventura, 2009), a seven-fold increase since 1960 (Coley, 2001). When children are born without the legal benefit of the protection and commitment marriage affords, fathers who have good intentions at the start (Johnson, 2000) gradually decrease their involvement over time. Of unmarried fathers, about half regularly have contact with their children in the first few years, but by school age, the rate decreases to 20–35% (Furstenberg & Harris, 1993). Divorce apparently speeds the process; one-third of divorced fathers have no contact with their children (Nord & Zill, 1996). How are these children affected?

Answers from research on single-parenting are ambiguous. And that's probably because there are multiple factors involved in single parenting. Although there seems to be a connection between living with a single parent and teen pregnancy and dropping out of school, many children have additional relationships that help protect them from these fates. Father's absence is important, and the presence of a stepfather or other biological relative does not necessarily improve the child's chances (McLanahan & Sandefur, 1994). So, what does? Let's look at the assumptions underlying the grim predictions for children of single parents.

Many homes headed by single mothers are economically poor; at least 40% are below poverty level (US Census Bureau, 2008). The lack or loss of income to a family affects where children live and go to school, and so influences whom they spend time with, and how they spend that time. In Harris' view (1998), poverty's most important effect on children is their status with peers. Not only do they lack the advantages others assume as their rights (e.g. good healthcare, music lessons, sporting equipment) but often they never even consider attending college because no one they know has considered it. However, not all the negative effects of single parenting are explained by economics. Although many single parents do an incredible job even with the dual pressures of defying cultural expectations and stretching one income, the contributions of a second parent cannot be dismissed as merely a matter of conforming to the norm or providing a comfortable living.

What seems to matter for the child is the quality of the relationship they come to expect, or *not* to expect, from a father. Having a toxic relationship with father, or one that decreased in closeness, is more harmful than no relationship at all (Furstenberg & Harris, 1993). Young children are very adaptable and their expectations are still forming, so an early separation may be easier for the young child than the older one. The child who has had many years of framing a relationship with father is likely to be very disillusioned with an absent dad and confused by the failure of the model they created for father–child relationship. Thus, the father who helps the child to scaffold a positive relationship over many years and then fails to follow through is a huge disappointment for the child of divorce or separation. And mothers will have trouble filling that gap.

But what of homes headed by single fathers? The number of single-father families is much fewer, and less likely to be poor. That seems to give them a positive edge. Families headed by single fathers report greater cohesion and higher adaptability than found in traditional families (Hatfield & Abrams, 1995). Overall, these fathers communicated more frequently with their children than did traditional fathers. Given that there are so few fathers who choose (or are given the choice) to single-parent, it may be that these men feel particularly drawn to parenting and feel competent to meet its demands.

So, can we conclude that single parenting is detrimental to a child's development? Not necessarily. If it means the child will live in poverty, the answer is devastatingly yes. If it means the child's expectations for one parent–child relationship are crushed, the answer is probably yes. But many successful and satisfied children emerge from single-parent homes, so they do not spell disaster across the board. But single parents would be wise to consider how they will handle alone the communication processes detailed in the rest of this chapter.

Children's communication in post-divorce families can be further complicated by the fact that, in joint custody arrangements, some children must live in two households simultaneously: in a **bi-residential** situation. Bi-residential co-parented children face a complex and difficult situation as they learn to adapt to at least two systems of rules as well as a variety of roles (rules and roles are discussed in the next chapters). To put it simply, they must constantly adapt to two family cultures and reorganize their own lives and relationships accordingly. What makes for effective post-divorce, bi-residential co-parenting? Authoritative parenting styles, continued communication of warmth towards the child, maintaining mutual interest and mutual involvement in the child's life, responsiveness to the child's growing needs, as well as effective management of conflict all contribute to functional post-divorce, bi-residential co-parenting (Lewis, Johnson-Reitz, & Wallerstein, 2004).

But co-parenting also requires adjustments. Co-parents must renegotiate the boundaries of intimacy, power and access (Emery

& Dillon, 1994). Co-parents often use the divorce decree as either a legal contract or as a set of less formal guidelines to structure post-divorce communication (Schrodt, Baxter, McBride, Braithwaite, & Fine, 2006) although everyday interactions eventually become brief and informal (Braithwaite, McBride, & Schrodt, 2003). The family restructuring continues if either parent remarries, as we shall see below (under *stepfamilies*).

Custodial Grandparenting

Although this could be yet another form of single-parent family, it is more often the case that one or both parents are also sheltered in a grandparents' home, so it usually becomes an extended family unit in which grandparents provide much of the nurturance that parents would traditionally give. Adults who return to their childhood homes, with or without their children, are referred to as **boomerang children** (Vogl-Bauer, 2009), and they have become more numerous. Grandparent-headed homes increased 76% from 1970 to 1997 (Casper & Bryson cited in Goodman & Silverstein, 2001). Although this sort of arrangement was most common among African Americans, it was found as well among Hispanics and non-Hispanic whites (Saluter, 1996). Given recent increases in unemployment and home foreclosures, the numbers of boomerang children and their children are probably even greater now. This arrangement apparently provides more stability for children, but the effects are often less than satisfactory for parents and grandparents (Solomon & Marx, 1995).

Among African-American custodial grandparents, there are problems with keeping paid employment and finding downtime (Burton, 1992). In general, grandparents who take on the parenting role reported lower satisfaction with grandparenting and a reduced sense of wellbeing (Shore & Hayslip, 1995). One of the problems seems to be that the expectations for all parties are unclear in this situation. Grandparents' roles must shift to provide parenting, while parents must relinquish some of their normal duties to grandparents. Furthermore, most custodial grandparenting is in response to distress in the nuclear family. Goodman and Silverstein

(2001) found that most of the grandmothers they spoke to cared for their grandchildren because of some dysfunction in the middle-generation parents: drug addiction was high on the list (74.5%), followed by abuse or neglect of the grandchildren (33.6%), and a few cases of parent death, illness, or incarceration.

When the triad of grandparent, parent, and child are equally linked in these configurations, then most parties are satisfied (Vogl-Bauer, 2009). These connected-triads typically mean optimal parental involvement as well as hope for the eventual resumption of the parental role. According to Goodman and Silverstein (2001), when grandmother is the link between child and parent, she expresses high satisfaction. However, when the child is the link between parent and grandparent, grandmother expresses lower satisfaction. But what is most important (but not the subject of research) is that this middle position is probably very unhealthy for the child. If the appropriate authoritative party – the grandparent who is the caregiver – links the family triad, then outcomes are fairly positive. But most grandparents would prefer simply to be grandparents – to have the freedom to spoil their grandchildren and still have their own adult lives.

Polygamous Parent Families

Polygamy (multiple marital partnerships) has been a dominant form of family worldwide until fairly recent times (Valsiner, 1989) and about 80% of world cultures have allowed some version of it. **Polygyny** (one husband, several wives) is the most frequent form; whereas **polyandry** (one wife, several husbands) and **polygynandry** (group marriage) are found only in certain cultures near the Indian subcontinent (Valsiner, 1989). When we look into this family configuration, we may be prepared to find it lacking. As most fans of the nuclear family will tell you, the only thing worse than having too few parents is having too many. Turns out, it is not that simple.

Despite our cultural reservations about this family form, there are advantages, especially for children. Valsiner (1989) reports several differences between children from monogamic and polygynic families. One particularly significant for communication is that they have more opportunities to observe adult–adult interaction among various small group configurations in addition to the usual interpersonal dyads of mother–father. Another difference is that children observe more changes in family composition (new wives, births and deaths of siblings) and that undoubtedly leaves the child more resilient in the face of loss but perhaps less securely attached to a primary caregiver. Of course, social support is abundant with multiple wives; the child continues to receive care even if the birth mother is absent.

Consider the effects on interaction and relationships of having multiple mothers. In a monogamic family, the child can only influence two adults and often learns to play one against the other. In a polygynic family, the child has fewer opportunities to influence the husband–wife relationship because of the decreased dependence between the two when there are other co-wives. Most interesting, the child has greater opportunity to develop peer relationships at home. Not only are there more siblings to choose from, but also the odds are better that a child will have a sibling close in age (Valsiner, 1989). Thus, the child in a polygynic family simply has a richer interaction environment *at home* than a child in a monogamic family typically has. However, there's an argument to be made that our culturally approved form of serial monogamy (divorce and remarriage) can provide the same richness. However, blended families and stepfamilies have their own dynamics.

Stepfamilies and Blended Families

Stepfamily traditionally has meant "at least two adults who provide continued care for at least one child who is not the biological offspring of both adults" (Turner & West, 2002, p. 25). Most recently, there is a move toward the less freighted term **blended family** so as to emphasize the integration of new members to the family unit as well as the diversity of these families' configurations (Baxter, Braithwaite, & Nicholson, 1999). No matter what term we use, a reorganization of family members and communication dynamic is inevitable when living arrangements change.

In the early years of stepfamily development, as when divorced or widowed parents remarry, they may be unprepared for the key difference for children: a new adult to the system is "stepping in" to assume responsibility for nurturing another person's child (Coleman, Ganong, & Fine, 2004; Juroe & Juroe, 1983). Knowing what we do about attachment in early life and the fact that a child internalizes parental values, emotional expression, and communication patterns, a smooth "stepping in" to someone else's parental role is unlikely. Add that to the fact that a step-parent relationship is imposed on a child, unlike the chosen marriage relationship, and problems begin.

Some families handle the inevitable tensions of "blending" gracefully and some do not. Handling this tension between the child's forced adaptation and the parents' free choice is a two-step process (Cissna, Cox, & Bochner, 1990). The first step is to establish the solidity of the marriage by setting some general rules for the reorganization of the family. That the remarried parents have formed a coalition is a matter of direct communication in their wedding vows. How they then communicate that commitment to their children and how the children interpret it may be a more complicated matter. The second step is to establish the credibility of the step-parent as an authority (Cissna et al., 1990). This means not only that the natural parent must trust the step-parent's abilities, but the child must trust them as well. Later in the chapter, we will examine a model of family dialectics characterized by authority/autonomy and love/hostility. In blended families these dialectical tensions may be strained: "The internal dialectic between love and affection on the one hand and discipline and authority on the other is especially problematic in the stepfamily" (Cissna et al., 1990, p. 56). Children may find it very difficult to adapt to the love and authority demands of new adults in a culturally normative family.

Children, faced with new family members and roles, make sense of the stepfamily in a variety of ways. Schrodt (as cited in Braithwaite, Schrodt, & Baxter, 2006) identified themes of stepfamily functioning based on inventories completed by adult and adolescent stepchildren. Stepfamilies were seen in terms of their levels of dissension, avoidance, expressiveness, involvement, and flexibility. The way that children think about their stepfamilies helps distinguish strong (high involvement, expressiveness, and flexibility) from problematic stepfamilies (high dissension and avoidance), although children identified a range of five kinds of stepfamilies from bonded (high functioning) to conflictual (low functioning). Children form schemes for making sense of the new stepfamily based, at least in part, on how parents manage the shift. But they also must take into account the contradictory impulses they feel.

Children face three contradictions in the step-parent–stepchild relationship: (1) children desire both emotional closeness and distance with the step-parent; (2) they want a relationship, but often reject closeness in the interests of loyalty to the non-residential parent; (3) they want family authority to rest with their residential parent, but also want the parent and step-parent to share authority (Baxter, Braithwaite, Bryant, & Wagner, 2004). We will return to the dialectical tensions in families later in this chapter. Sufficient for now is the knowledge that children in blended families face more complex relational tasks than those in nuclear families. But what is happening in other family configurations? Do children of alternative families experience different kinds of problems?

Same-Sex Parent Families

Even early estimates of the number of young children with at least one gay parent run into the low millions (Bozett, 1987; Gottman, 1990), so quite a few children are affected by our cultural preference for and legal sanction of the husband–wife configuration. Of late, homosexual parents have challenged the interpretation of the "best interests of the child" as placement with biological parents (see Patrick & Palladino, 2009). Courts may base their decisions on the argument that homosexual parenting models problematic behavior for a child's socialization, in particular their socialization into gender and sexual roles (Allen & Burrell, 1996). Is this a well-founded argument?

In a comparison of children of lesbian mothers and single,

heterosexual women, there were no significant differences among boys (Green, Mandel, Hotvedt, Gray, & Smith, 1986). Although girls of lesbian mothers dressed and played in less traditionally feminine ways, none of them suffered a disorder of gender identity. And there were basically no differences between the parenting skills of heterosexual parents and gay and lesbian parents (Clay, 1990). In 1996, Allen and Burrell summarized studies done before 1995, based on reports from both adults and children, and found virtually no difference between homosexual and heterosexual parenting. Although children's reports showed no difference between those with gay or straight parents regarding life satisfaction and sexual orientation, those with homosexual parents demonstrated slight advantages in moral and cognitive development. So, although our current mores may define homosexuality as criminal (in some parts of the US), sexual preference has little bearing on parenting. As Basile (1974) put it, "The best interests of the child lay with a loving parent, not with a heterosexual parent or a homosexual parent" (p. 18). Further, there is evidence that in states that allow foster parenting by gay and lesbian couples, not only are children faring well, but gay and lesbian couples are helping states to alleviate problems in obtaining care for older, troubled, unwanted children (Patrick & Palladino, 2009).

Weston (1991) points out in *Families We Choose* that gay families have been defined by contrast with straight families. But, she makes the case that **created families** run the gamut and are qualitatively different from biological families in their nature as chosen commitments. Voluntary families are not necessarily just gay families, but can include communes, kibbutzim, and collectives based on religion, age, or convenience. For example, the founding mother of the Grey Panthers, Maggie Kuhn, followed her commitment to bridging the age gap among generations and opened her home to welcome a voluntary family of all ages. Thus, the notion of family is expanding to include any collective of humans that fulfills needs for intimacy, support, enrichment, development, and companionship. There are many kinds of families; all are agents of potential.

Regardless of the configuration into which the child is born,

Families Communicating with Children

every family of every type engages in communication processes essential to the management of the nurturing group. We look next at some of these processes.

Family-Group Communication Processes

Among the many communication processes to which children are exposed as they interact in families, group communication figures prominently. **Group task processes** (processes that pertain to goal-directed activities such as making decisions, solving problems, and leadership) will be covered later in Chapter 5. Here, we focus on **group social processes** that pertain to family-group relationships, specifically, cohesiveness (closeness–distance) and climate (warmth–coldness).

Cohesiveness. Within everyday family-group interactions there are moments when members feel psychologically close as well as moments where they feel distant. In general, **cohesiveness** "describes the psychological closeness a group's members feel toward one another" (Scheerhorn & Geist, 1997), or what family scholars refer to as "emotional bonding" (Galvin, Bylund, & Brommel, 2008, p. 30). Almost all models of family functioning (such as the Circumplex Model of Olson, Russell, & Sprenkle, 1983) incorporate cohesiveness as a continuum that includes: disengagement (extreme separateness), separateness (emotional independence, some involvement), connectedness (joint involvement and some individuality), and enmeshment (extreme closeness, almost no individuality) (see Galvin, Bylund, & Brommel, 2008; Olson et al., 1983).

The cohesion models acknowledge that "optimal cohesion" is culturally based [some cultures preferring closeness (e.g. Hispanic, Mediterranean, etc.); others preferring distance (e.g. British)], interpreted and redefined by individual families, and is also a moving target insofar as family members' perceptions of family

Disengagement ------- Separateness ------- Connectedness ------- Enmeshment
(absolute individuality)   (no individuality)

Figure 3.1 Cohesiveness Continuum

60

cohesion can change as they interact as well as over time. Although we are not aware of attempts in the research literature to formally link models of family functioning and infant attachment processes (as discussed in earlier chapters), it would seem that for infants and young children, families functioning in the connectedness–enmeshment range of the cohesiveness scale would offer an optimal developmental context. And, much later, families with adolescents might fare better in the connected–separated range on the continuum (allowing for increasing autonomy while remaining connected). In any case, optimal family functioning in the US typically finds members to be in the mid-range of cohesiveness: feeling close with a nod to individuality.

For children, cohesiveness is learned through family interactions where, for example, living in close proximity to relatives, regular family telephone calls from members of the immediate unit as well as extended family, regular family gatherings, frequent positive physical contact among members (kisses, hugs), regular retellings of family stories at meals, celebratory rituals (holidays, birthdays, etc.), reviewing family photo albums depicting family events, and more provide communication lessons of family connectedness–enmeshment. The extent to which children learn to feel connected to their immediate family unit (whatever configuration that might be) as well as the extended family depends on regular, positive episodes of family communication. Of course, the absence of these kinds of family communication episodes, and/or experiencing reoccurring episodes of negative family interaction teaches children the merits of keeping distant. Understand that each family will find its own level of cohesion, and for some, low cohesion is either a result of lack of contact opportunities (competing work schedules, physical distance from extended family members) or of their own expectations and preferences (cultural or otherwise).

Climate. Like weather, **family climate** refers to family members' "perceptions of the relative warmth or coldness that characterizes the interpersonal relationships among members" (Scheerhorn & Geist, 1997, p. 91). And like weather it can change, however, if a climate is experienced regularly it can form lasting impressions.

As a young child, for example, Tom can recall entering his

maternal grandparents apartment and being greeted by scents of chocolate-chip cookies baking and lemon furniture polish, seeing colorful sofas and chairs, and hearing his maternal grandmother, Mae, say, "Hi ya, Tommy!" He also recalls entering another relative's home and being greeted by the odors and barking of a poodle, seeing furniture covered in thick plastic, and hearing a distant male relative say, "Hi (to the adults). Come in." And to Tom and his brothers "Boys, leave the dog alone. Take off your shoes. Why don't you go to the basement and try to not make a mess." Needless to say Tom was less than excited to visit this particular relative's home, but looked forward to visiting his grandparents as often as he could. The difference, in part, was due to perceptions of family climate: one was warm and inviting and the other cold and unwelcoming (at least to Tom).

Creating a warm, child-friendly family climate is of course important in part because recurring climate can form a lasting impression (Tom's memories are of events that occurred at least 45 years ago). But such a climate also contributes to positive family communication processes. For example, Tom cannot recall ever hearing his maternal grandparents, Mae and Harry, whom he visited at least twice each week, raise their voices, speak harshly, use inappropriate language (unless in fun), or say anything that was hurtful or demeaning. Communication with his grandparents was always warm, easy, validating, and comfortable, and remained so over the course of their lives (Mae and Harry were married for over 70 years, lived into their early 90s, and in their later years lived with and were cared for by Tom's mother, Mary, and father, Jim). Just like the household in which Tom grew up with his parents and two brothers, grandma and grandpa's home was a place to share ideas, be heard, loved, and of course, to eat. What are your memories of your childhood family's climate? In what ways might climate have affected your communication development?

Within family units there are many kinds of relationships that provide children with many different kinds of opportunities to learn about relational communication. Let's take a closer look at some of the significant ones.

Children's Communication and Family Relationships

Biological Mothers and Fathers

Although this relationship does not include the child, it certainly influences the child. And the child influences the relationship between parents. Indeed, the arrival of the first baby subjects the couple to a period of stress and adaptation. With the constant attention a new baby requires, communication between spouses declines. In the first two years of marriage, both parents and non-parents experience less marital satisfaction, as well as fewer shared activities and positive interactions (MacDermid, Huston, & McHale, 1990). The difference between the two groups is that parents' activities became more child-oriented and the division of household tasks became more traditional. The latter may violate many young mothers' expectations for the marriage relationship. Tasks may have been shared more or less equally before the baby's arrival, but new fathers often become less involved in home responsibilities, and this puts a damper on the young mother's view of marriage (Belsky, Ward, & Rovine, 1986).

The demands of infant caregiving can be overwhelming to a new parent. Over half of new parents reported problems with infant nutrition and illness; only 10% of problems involved marital and role conflicts (McKim, as cited in Mebert, 1991). As with other family configuration shifts, such as blended families, parents who prepare well, plan the change (in this case, pregnancy), and create similar internal models of the family beforehand are those who make the transition gradually and well (Mebert, 1991).

Parent and Child

The relationship between mother and child is often idealized as the perfect bond embodying unconditional love. If all is well with the child's health and capacities for interaction and all is well with mother's willingness to be communicatively responsive, then that lovely secure attachment ensues. But a newborn's illness or premature birth can affect his or her capacity to interact; a mother's postpartum depression or family distress can influence how present she can be for her baby. Interventions can help bring mother and child together in these cases, but they must be immediate to forestall subsequent deterioration of the relationship. What we don't know for sure is whether father can provide an equally good attachment partner. We know that mothers and fathers seem to parent slightly differently, but are alike in their affectionate behavior. As we saw in earlier chapters, the relationship between father and child provides material and emotional support, models gender role expectations and physical play, and scaffolds family communication norms. What does the child learn to expect from these parental behaviors?

Children develop expectations for parents on the basis of what parents' model for them. And the more parents then continue to meet children's expectations, the more satisfied children are (Dixson, 1995). Most importantly, the more family members encourage honest communication and accept disagreement, the higher the child's reported satisfaction and the smaller the difference between expectation and experience. Dixson interprets this to mean that a child who perceives an open family environment is a child who is able to challenge perceived inadequacies. The model set up for family relationship rules can be brought out into the open zone (of proximal development) with the parent so it may be clarified, explained, and possibly adjusted. The relationship story can be expressed aloud and therefore inform the model being constructed internally. If communication is suppressed, models remain internal standards that are unmet and thus end in dissatisfaction.

We have known little about children's models for the parent–child relationship until Dixson and Stein (1997) polled 88 children, ages 6 to 12, about how parents and children are supposed to feel and behave, and the rules they should use to interact. Girls expect to go places with parents (to eat, to shop, on vacations) and to adhere to communication rules (don't interrupt, talk nice). Boys think children should be emotionally supportive with parents (cheer them up, give hugs and kisses). Other research confirms that girls emphasize communication rules more than boys, but the boys' focus on emotional supportiveness may contradict stereotypes about gender roles. Over the developmental course, both boys' and girls' models developed away from instrumental needs (they should take care of me) to more social and emotional needs (they should help me feel better, take me to parties) (Dixson & Stein, 1997). So, it would appear that parents and children use relational models that share some common elements, such as social and emotional support.

Siblings

One of the benefits of developing in a large family is that some communication skills are learned from and practiced with siblings. That effect has something to do with birth order as well. The youngest of five siblings in Julie's family did not utter true words for the first year and a half of his life. A concerned Mrs Yingling consulted the pediatrician who wisely asked, "How does he get what he wants?" She responded, "He grunts and one of his older siblings gets it for him." He concluded, "Why should he work if someone else will do it for him?" As the story goes, he began to speak in sentences pretty soon thereafter.

When siblings greet a new arrival, they do so with reservations. Another child draws on limited parental resources, meaning less of everything for the older siblings. On the other hand, the new baby will get less of parents' attentions than the older ones did. Mothers of multiple children will be more likely to interact with their infant in the presence of other siblings rather than one-on-one, and they use less metalinguistic speech with their younger children than do mothers of only children (Jones & Adamson, 1987). However, infants who must vie for attention with other siblings take more turns in multiple-member interactions than during one-to-one interaction with either mother alone or sibling alone (Barton & Tomasello, 1991). Thus, younger siblings typically learn some of the trickier rules of social interaction earlier because of the challenges siblings provide. Parents provide careful scaffolding; siblings provide no such coddling so the toddler learns to deal with life's insults in a somewhat protected environment. Older siblings begin to tease toddlers as early as 18 months, and that teasing increases, becoming more verbal and explicit over time (Dunn & Munn, 1985).

Students are always interested in birth-order effects – in particular, how it has affected their own families! Let's be clear here that although birth order certainly seems to bear upon family dynamics, it is the relational dynamic *within* a family that has more bearing on outcomes like temperament, intelligence, and personality than simple sibling position *across* families. For example, Julie's youngest brother, simply by virtue of his birth position, should have scored lower on IQ tests than his older siblings. But he didn't; his score was the highest among the five. According to his older siblings, that's because they taught him everything they know. Hmm. Maybe. Stay tuned – we will discuss birth order (as a family role) in Chapter 4.

Step-parent and Child

As demonstrated above, the blended family experiences a transition period during which communication rules and roles must be adapted for the new configuration. Some families move more smoothly than others. In the first four years of blended family history, the most frequent transition or "turning point" had to do with changes in household composition, such as remarriage, cohabitation, and children's visits (Baxter, Braithwaite, & Nicholson, 1999). Next frequent were conflict transitions, followed by reconciliation points, then the more positively valued holidays and quality-time events. Baxter and her colleagues (1999) found five trajectories for blended family development, the most frequent two being patterns that led to high levels of "feeling like a family," one very rapid with positive turning points, and one slower with gradual movement to family feeling. The third most common was the dramatic and unstable "high-amplitude turbulent" for its "roller coaster effect" of rapid increases and rapid decreases in "feeling like a family." The last two ended the four-year period at low levels of family feeling; one stagnated at the start, and the other started at high levels but declined through a series of negative turning points.

Once the new family order is established, what can a child and step-parent expect? Much of the research on child–step-parent communication has been conducted with adolescents; that may be because they are the most available and numerous children of divorce. Teens make many decisions about who to talk to, about what topics. They avoid talking about sex with any sort of parent, but avoid many more topics with step-parents: money issues, the biological parent, really, any deep topic (Golish & Caughlin, 2002). Talking with step-parents is deemed risky, perhaps for fear of being trapped in the middle between parent and step-parent conflict. Children will generally protect the parental relationship even at the risk of alienating the step-parent. The wise step-parent will recognize the primacy of the biological parent bond and remain open, biding time and topic until the child senses a low-risk opportunity to interact.

Grandparent and Grandchild

Most grandparents are not obligated to serve as full-time care-givers, so it is typically a less duty-bound family position than others. We still expect grandparents to link the generations, however, despite "the new social contract" (Kornhaber & Woodward, 1981) in which "no one is obliged to anyone else" (p. 97). Grandparenting styles run the gamut as a result of this more open-ended set of social expectations, from detached or passive to supportive or influential (Cherlin & Furstenberg, 1986). Grandparent roles can vary with gender role, age, employment status, marital status, and educational level (Robertson, 1977).

Because grandparenting is less firmly defined than it once was, and our culture is more mobile, grandparents are often far away from grandchildren, so they can feel some ambivalence about their roles (Wood, V.,1982). Disconnected grandparents often express regret about their failure to pass on family history, and their grandchildren feel frustration and anger at the lack of connection to elders and the gap in their ability to predict their own future aging process (Kornhaber & Woodward, 1981). On the other hand, those connected grandparents who have close relationships with grandchildren are also more likely to be socially involved, enjoy good mental health, and maintain a sense of pride in their grandchildren (Lin & Harwood, 2003).

Several factors influence the development of relationships between grandchildren and grandparents: acceptance of the grandparenting role, physical proximity among the generations, parental divorce, and the quality of the relationship between parent and grandparent (Nussbaum, Pecchioni, Robinson, & Thompson, 2000). What seems to count is the sheer amount of time grandparents are likely to spend with grandchildren. When frequent interactions are the rule, the relationships are marked by feelings of significance and satisfaction (Kornhaber & Woodward, 1981). Additionally, children who have frequent interaction with older adults may have fewer age-related prejudices (Hickey, Hickey, & Kalish, 1968); and those with close grandparents tend to use positive stereotypes for them (Pecchioni & Croghan, 2002).

Despite the finding above that physical proximity is one important factor in the grandparent–grandchild relationship, communication media may supplement or substitute for proximity. Telephone communication is apparently quite satisfactory, and frequent use of e-mail is also linked to close grandparent–grandchild relationships (Holladay & Siepke, 2003, as cited in Floyd & Morman, 2006, pp. 72–73). Considering the increased mobility of older adults and their growing use of electronic media, the Internet has great potential for building positive relationships between grandparents and grandchildren (Harwood, 2004).

By the time children are in college, those with involving and satisfying relationships with grandparents saw them as attentive, supportive, affectionate, respectful, and sharing (Harwood, 2000). The strongest negative predictor for the relationship was grandparents' over-accommodation – the perception that the grandparent talked down to them or negatively stereotyped young people. So, the grandparent who can find some ease with grandchildren, adapt to their changes as they grow, and respect them as individuals will continue to enjoy the benefits of active grandparenting. The primary benefit seems to be a sense of continuity: the chance to reconnect with the past, to interpret life experiences in stories for the younger generation, and to thereby build a coherent whole (McKay, 1993). Constructing a narrative of one's life for grandchildren not only establishes the grandparent as a guide, but also confirms the integrity of the grandparent's past, links it to the present they share, and to the future they will not.

By now, you know that every family relationship has its tensions and points of negotiation as well as its joys and moments of fulfillment. Now we turn to examine those tensions through the lens of **relational dialectics**.

Managing Family Relational Dialectics with Social Communication Skills

Relational Dialectics

Dialectical processes are found in every relationship of any significance. Although most social sciences acknowledge **dialectics,** we'll focus here on those that function in relationships. The two principles underlying dialectics are process and contradiction. You may already be familiar with the notion of process, or "the ongoing dynamics that affect how relationships develop and change over time," while contradiction focuses on "interdependency and interaction among competing needs, desires, and feelings" (Wood, J. T., 2000, p. 44). The three contradictions common to personal relationships are: autonomy/connection–competing needs for independence and interdependence, novelty/predictability–competing needs for stimulation and routine, and openness/closedness–competing needs to share one's private thoughts or feelings and to maintain privacy (Baxter & Montgomery, 1996). Dialectic refers to the inevitable contradiction between poles of oppositional needs – inevitable because each pole relies on the opposing pole. Let's take an example. You've all heard (or said) at some point, "I'm so bored" (often from a child nearing the middle of summer vacation!) However, if you stripped the child of all routine, of all expected events in their day (breakfast, bathing, a mix of play and work, family dinner conversation, bedtime story) then novelty would have no meaning – all would be chaos and confusion. So, we need the routine to recognize the novelty. We need the novelty to appreciate the routine. The tension lies between simultaneously competing desires; we want both.

These relationship dialectics are at work in family relationships too. Because of the special nature of family relationships, you will find the names of the dialectics may vary a bit, but they bear some similarity to the ones we've introduced above. Featured in families, you will find a love/hostility dialectic that does not fit easily into the three relational dialectics, but seems to be a characteristic tension nonetheless. With relatives, we often don't have the option of walking away, yet we still have strong feelings to manage. This dialectic may then affect how we handle the other tensions.

Family Dialectics

Integration/differentiation. One way of looking at how several family dialectics work is to use the distinction between a simple and a complex family. A **complex family** is both highly integrated and highly differentiated, whereas a **simple family** system is low on both ends of the dialectic. As Rathunde and Csikszentmihalyi (1991) explain: "Integration allows family members to maintain relations with others through shared investment" whereas differentiation "allows an individual to construct a separate self through having the control to invest in personal goals" (p. 144). Notice that the dialectic of autonomy and control (see below) enters the complexity equation as well. Parents in complex homes help their children discover the rewards of pursuing goals (autonomously) by being vigilant about what interests them, what bores them, what makes them anxious. In these homes, thoughts and feelings are more transparent than in simple families, so potentials may be optimized (p. 158). Such parents want their children to reach their individual potentials, but also want close family relationships. They achieve those seemingly competing goals by being authoritative parents using an open communication style.

Autonomy/control. This dialectic overlaps somewhat with the one above. A family characterized by high differentiation will be comprised of members who can act autonomously as well as together, therefore have little need to control another's behavior but great need to control their own. A simple family will try to control family members to attempt to get their needs met, but in the process reveal their dependence on others for their own feelings of worth. For example, let's say mother is thinking of returning to work after her youngest is in preschool. In a complex family, she will express her wish to work, her feelings of anxiety about re-entering the workforce, and her reservations about leaving home and children. Her family, wanting her to be autonomous *and* integrated, expresses understanding for her mixed feelings, appreciation for her concern, and then urges her to give it a try after everyone is comfortable with how the baby is adapting to preschool. In a simple family, she may have similar feelings, but does not express them. She announces she wants to work and will expect everyone to help more around the house. Husband and children, probably feeling pushed away, neglected, and unimportant to her, respond that they cannot allow it and she must not do it. Both sides attempt to control; both sides end by feeling needy and inadequate.

Intimacy/detachment. As we already know, children need a stable attachment with their caregiver; a solid place to stand and face the world. If all goes well, the child's first interactions are with willingly responsive caregivers who provide affection, attention and support. This child is provided the framework of a loving, welcoming family and becomes a person who enjoys and trusts other people. On the other hand, some children's first interaction experiences are with neglectful, dismissive, and unresponsive caregivers, and the likely result will be a person who is anxious or dismissive with others. Most people will experience both ends of the dialectic and learn to manage them competently. Everyone eventually meets an unresponsive person, or occasionally experiences a frazzled parent who is dismissive. And everyone reaches a point in a relationship when the intimacy becomes overwhelming and they need some detachment. A very simple example is the

71

newborn that definitely needs and wants interaction and touch, but cannot yet manage a lot of stimulation. So, if father talks and plays for too long, the infant has ways – turning away, going to sleep, and crying – of turning off the stimulation, of detaching. As with all dialectics, this is a tension between opposing forces that everyone feels and must learn to manage.

Love/hostility. One widespread cultural assumption is that family members love one another, and in particular, that parents love children. However, without the possibility for hostility, there would be no love but merely a vaguely positive sentiment without a defining counterpoint. When we are so close to another that we allow them to know us deeply and to integrate and become interdependent with us, we have opened the door for both love and hostility. Think about it; you are rarely openly hostile with strangers or people you don't really care about. "You always hurt the one you love" has some truth to it. Children, in particular, often express hostility to their parents when their autonomous desires are thwarted. It may be jarring to hear a 3-year-old say, "I hate you, Mommie" but it is a sign that, not only does he also feel love, but he is developing a sense of his personal power as a being separate from mother.

Psychologists have identified various types of love. Sternberg's (1986) triangular theory of love included three dimensions: passion, intimacy, and commitment. Combinations of the three dimensions yield various types of love, for example, intimacy and passion result in the familiar romantic love, and closeness and commitment result in companionate love. **Consummate love,** the result of combining all three dimensions (high passion, high intimacy, and high commitment), is the most durable type, and is the kind of love that we would expect to experience in optimal parent–child relationships. From a positive communication vantage point (and framed dialectically), families communicating consummate love convey passion (versus detachment), closeness (versus distance), and commitment (versus indifference) in everyday family interactions.

Open/closed. All parents expect their children to tell them the truth, to be honest with them. And are they? Well, not always. And here's why. Once a child recognizes the power of the negative at around two years, the world of possibility opens up to them, and they realize that they can represent what is *not* as well as what *is*. If you ask a 2-year-old if she wants a cookie, she just might say "no" to make herself giggle (while holding out her hand for the cookie). "No" has great power to change the world and to retain control for self. It also means the beginning of dissembling. When a child begins to be able to think silently and speak socially, she can figure out what words would please mother. And sometimes those words bear little resemblance to reality. It seems easy enough at age 7 for Jacque to tell father that he did his homework if it means he gets to go to the ballpark. Adolescents have more complicated reasons that involve protecting a private sense of self. By the teen years, most children have begun to challenge parental authority even with the most benign parents. One of the tasks of adolescence is to develop moral reasoning, and that can mean questioning social conventions. All this is to the good as it helps improve perspective-taking (Paikoff & Brooks-Gunn, 1991). However, if parents have trouble accepting their children's growing needs for personal control, they can thwart not only their developing identities but their newly forming system of morality as well. Then a downward spiral can occur: If parents cannot tolerate open discussion, children have fewer opportunities to take their perspectives about social norms, thus may give in and comply with parents' demands with no understanding or internalizing of the underlying values. And of course, unpleasantly hostile verbal arguments can take the place of open communication and distress the relationship and the family (Canary, Cupach, & Messman, 1995).

The wise parent knows that disclosure is a dialectical phenomenon; the potential discloser must decide whether to reveal or conceal (Dindia, 1998). And access rules for disclosure involve selecting safe and secure situations and listeners. Unless parents give permission for children to tell them about nonconforming or non-preferred behaviors, they are unlikely to hear about them. Providing safe settings and open communication increases the likelihood of revelations from teens. Then, the parents' responses should be attentive and nonjudgmental. Easy? No, not at all.

Worth practicing? Oh, yes. If the teen reveals that he is thinking about, oh, say, having sex with his girlfriend, it's likely he is talking through his own moral process and needs the open ear, rational questions, and calm feedback of a trustworthy person who loves him and respects him.

The dialectic of open/closed is particularly apparent in discussions about sex. How open should families be when communicating about sex? What should be kept private? From whom? Based on decades of research, Warren (1995) suggests that: (1) Parents should begin early to talk with children about sex as a part of teaching children to understand and care for their bodies. During a bath, for example, parents might name body parts, talk about respecting our bodies, and about privacy. (2) Parents should include appropriate discussions about sex within the many teachable moments of everyday family life. His research shows that parents typically discuss sex at the onset of puberty in a single episode referred to as "the talk." Of course, trying to teach all that we know about this significant topic in a single communication episode is absurd. And (3), family communication about sex is not the same thing as "sex education" (giving biological information). That is, as parents and children communicate about sex they are sharing values, attitudes, and beliefs about human sexuality, hopefully creating a supportive environment for continued learning about human sexuality, as well as sharing accurate biological information. And, as sexuality is of course a private family matter (contrary to how sex is portrayed on TV) it is also important to consider the matter of respecting privacy boundaries both inside and outside the family.

Parenting role dialectical model. One view of parent–child interactions describes a circular order of behaviors. Schaefer (1959, 1997) used a vertical axis between autonomy and control and a horizontal axis between hostility and love. If you sketch these two lines on one plane, you'll get four quadrants describing the possibilities of the parental role: love–control, control–hostility, hostility–autonomy, and autonomy–love. In conventional child–parent interaction, we favor behaviors in the control-love quadrant: nurturance and protectiveness.

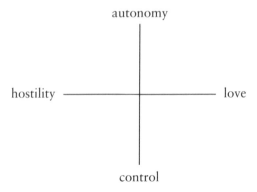

Figure 3.2

And as long as the child is dependent on parents, materially and emotionally, this is functional. However, the model works in circular fashion: parental love gives rise to protection and control, which the child will eventually resist, leading to hostility, parent relinquishing of control, and back again toward love.

Janet, for example, was the first sibling in her family to date quite a bit in high school. Dad always greeted dates at the door, and stayed up until she returned home. So far, that felt protective and loving. But Mom tended to be more accusing about suspected behavior. For example, when Janet practiced dancing in the basement with a boy, Mom feared their interaction went beyond dancing and said so in a disrespectful way ("The neighbors will think you're a tramp!") Hurt and self-protective, Janet went away to college vowing to share no information about romantic interests until she introduced a bridegroom. It took a very long time for her to realize that her parents soon relinquished the control–hostility quadrant of parenting, and were open to her romantic relationships far sooner than she had thought.

Child role dialectical model. Although we found no such model in the literature, we will take a stab at describing the dialectics children face in interaction with parents. Intimacy and detachment are quite clearly in play from the early bonding moments throughout a child's life as they struggle for the lovely closeness as well as the relief of detachment.

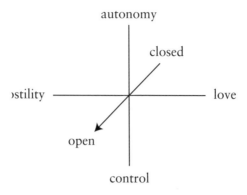

Figure 3.3

With detachment come the possibility of autonomy and its flip side of dependence. Young people must detach to start to explore who they are as autonomous beings, and in that process must struggle with the fact that they still depend on their parents for both affection and support. The words "As long as you're in my house, you'll (fill in the blank)" still ring in the ears of many owners of hard-won identities.

Finally, there is the open/closed dialectic we just explored. Every child starts out life as open as they can be; dissembling is impossible without symbols. But with the negative, and with the development of a separate self, some protection of that self becomes necessary. Parents, being those people who know you best early in life, are the prime targets for protection. So, how does all this look from the child's view?

Imagine the same grid as in the model for parenting, but with a third dimension: "open" toward the front in space, and "closed" toward the rear. Remember that no child will stay in one position; negotiating dialectics is a process of adjusting tensions. A child, then, must juggle complementary needs in at least eight child role spaces:

1. Autonomy – love–open. Herein lies the blessed position of being an independent self, openly expressing oneself, and maintaining the affection and support of parents. ("Ah, bliss!")

2. Autonomy – love–closed. This position is of a loved child who wants to be independent but feels he either cannot share or wants to draw a privacy boundary. ("They're great, but I've gotta do this alone.")
3. Love – control–open. In this space, the child again feels loved and loving, and acquiesces to the control of the parents in an open way; young children who have authoritative parents may often be here. ("I know you know best and I'm willing.")
4. Love – control–closed. In this case, the child acquiesces to control, loves the parents, but does not want to reveal to them; this could be the child who wants to be "good" but is not invited to share feelings and impulses. ("They think they know best, so I'll do what they want, even if I want something else.")
5. Control – hostility–open. Here is a space in which we find a child who is angry about the control wielded over him and doesn't mind saying so. ("I'll do it, but I won't like it!")
6. Control – hostility–closed. In this space we find the angry child who allows parents to call the shots, but does not reveal how he or she feels. This can happen with authoritarian parents, unwilling to listen to the child's feelings. ("I hate how they lord it over me; someday I'll grow up and be able to do just what I want.")
7. Autonomy – hostility–open. The child in this space is ready to be autonomous, angry, perhaps about attempted control, and is only too happy to let them know about it. ("I'm doing what I want and I'm going to let 'em have the truth.")
8. Autonomy – hostility–closed. From this position, the child ready to be independent has no intention of telling parents and is hostile to boot. This could describe the teenager who has been controlled for too long, probably by an authoritarian parent. To distinguish it from no. 6, this child is not going to acquiesce any longer. ("I'm going to do exactly what I want and never tell those control freaks!")

Well, that's a lot to track. But it serves to illustrate how complicated is the child's task in negotiating relationships with parents and why parents may want to establish rules for open communication, does it not? The child with parents who invite direct communication will navigate these dialectical tensions with the assistance of parents not only willing to share their own experiences, but eager to listen to the child's view. The above model is a guess, and needs to be tested. But it is safe to say that children generally have better developmental outcomes in a complex family with authoritative parents. Now we turn to some specific suggestions for promoting positive family experiences.

Promoting Learning about Positive Interactions in Relationships and Groups

In Chapter 6 we will offer recommendations about improving positive communication development at home, but for now let's briefly consider children's communication development in light of creating positive family relationships and family groups.

An important first task is to begin consciously to orient our messages towards positive outcomes, both personal and relational. For individuals, this means entering communication episodes thinking about the kinds of messages that might facilitate a partner's happiness, prompt positive cognitions (e.g. optimism), elicit positive emotions (e.g. joy), and support the valuing and expression of positive character strengths (e.g. kindness). For relationships, this means using communication to create mutual understanding, moments of shared happiness, an intrinsic valuing of the process of relating, and more. So, think positive communication!

It is important to understand, however, that using messages to prompt happiness is not the same as prompting pleasure. "**Pleasure** encompasses a family of subjective positive psychological states that range from 'raw feels of the body' . . . to higher pleasures of the mind occasioned by Beethoven's Ninth symphony . . ." (Peterson, 2006, p. 48). For children there are of course many activities that give them pleasure. (Recall Tom's Grandma's chocolate chip cookies? His mother Mary's cookies are even better! Sorry, Grandma.) Adults take for granted so many sights, sounds, smells, tastes, and textures that are new and pleasurable to children. To this day, for Tom, the smell of freshly cut grass cues many positive childhood memories of a favorite aunt, and good time with an uncle and aunt on their Iowa farm. What were your childhood pleasures? Eating a favorite food? Wearing a favorite article of clothing? Watching a favorite movie? How about your pleasures now? Anything carry over from childhood? How about pleasurable conversations? What makes conversations pleasurable for you?

There is nothing inherently problematic about experiencing life's pleasures and wanting children to do the same. However, experiencing pleasure is fleeting, momentary, and puts us on what positive psychologists refer to as a **hedonic treadmill**, where we quickly adapt to a pleasurable experience and then require more stimulation to return to the same level of satisfaction later on. Of course too much pleasure can become painful (eating too many cookies) as well as dulled into routine (Oh, not chocolate chip cookies again?)

Today, TV advertising has elevated pleasure to a kind of default state. Media scholar Neil Postman (1985) in *Amusing Ourselves to Death: Public Discourse in the Age of Show Business*, argues that we are surrendering our rights in exchange for constant entertainment that includes revising what was once news into "infotainment." So, you say that you are not experiencing pleasure as you read this section of this college-level textbook? How about we make the prose sizzle a bit more? Maybe, offer you a little toy of some kind as a reward for finishing reading this section? How about a frosty (or steaming) beverage as you read? Or, maybe our prose will read better on a beach in Tahiti? The trap of seeking pleasure is that it requires continued effort to maintain it, and when we quickly get used to something pleasurable on the hedonic treadmill, we need more of it, and more intense forms of it, in order to be satisfied. Prompting children's pleasure is important (although stay tuned for the marshmallow experiment in Chapter 4), however, we also need to think about how to prompt their happiness.

Discovering and using signature strengths to constitute moments of flow, especially in the service of others, is what positive psychologists have in mind when they think about authentic happiness (Seligman, 2002). While communicating to facilitate children's pleasure can be a bit tricky at times (as when hearing a moody child's retort, "But, I hate peanut butter sandwiches!"), it is a far easier task than prompting children's authentic happiness – a much more difficult task. It takes lots of communication to help children discover their strengths, and even more communication to orient them to using their talents in service of others. And, not all of these conversations will necessarily be pleasurable. Yet, this is exactly what optimal positive communication in families is about: using messages to help family members do what they do best, savor and celebrate their accomplishments, and support them when things are going awry.

For parents, prompting children's happiness means exposing children to a wide range of activities and helping them to discover activities that engage their attention and imagination over sustained periods of time. One important activity that can be both pleasurable (at times) and help to facilitate happiness is communication itself. Yes, communication can make you happy! Do you recall having conversations at home where time seemed to stop and you did not want the conversations to end? In Tom's childhood home, dinner conversations always seemed to prompt lengthy debates with his dad and brothers about an incredible and interesting array of topics. (Tom credits learning debate and argumentation skills first to his Dad, Jim, and later to a beloved Loyola University professor and mentor, Elaine Bruggemeier.) Although these family dinner discussions were sometimes heated, Tom and his family respected each other's opinions, and cared about each other – something that has not changed to this day in his family of origin or in his immediate family (with his wife, Diana and children Stephanie and Paul).

To help to move family relationships and groups to the positive side, communication must be counted among family values. In the next chapter we turn our attention to children learning structural aspects of family life: roles and rules.

Activities

1. Discuss the advantages and disadvantages of the nuclear family compared to other types of families (extended, polygamous,

voluntary). Have you, or anyone you know, had any experience with another form of family? Watch a few episodes of the HBO TV series, "Big Love." Do you think the children's roles and experiences are depicted realistically?

2. Have you or a close friend experienced life in a blended (step) family? Do you think the family was blended with adequate care and preparation? Of the five trajectories in the development of a blended family, which did yours follow? How might it have gone differently? Chart out a series of optimal alternate turning points that would have made the process smoother.

3. What do you think about the finding that boys, more so than girls, believe that children should provide emotional support to parents? How do you suppose boys develop such an expectation? And why do the girls focus on rules?

4. Consider the child who says she hates her mother. Does she also love her mother? What shifts in other dialectics might have affected her momentary choice of this pole?

5. Each person handles relational dialectics differently. Consider the extreme examples of each set of dialectics, and come up with a theory of what developmental experiences led to the extreme way of handling the dialectic. Start with the example of the extremes on autonomy/integration: (1) Jill, who simply cannot make a commitment and values her freedom to the point of excluding close relationships, and (2) Jack, who needs to be with his intimate partner, and if he cannot, he gets anxious and calls his friends looking for company. Make a guess as to what sort of attachment they had with parents, as well as what communication style was employed in their families when they were young.

Suggested Further Reading

Dunn, J. (1993). *Young children's close relationships: Beyond attachment.* Newbury Park, CA: Sage.

Planalp, S. (1999). *Communicating emotion: Social, moral, and cultural processes.* Paris: Cambridge University Press.

Rosenberg, M. B. (2005). *Raising children compassionately: Parenting the nonviolent communication way.* Encinitas, CA: PuddleDancer Press.

4

———————

Children Learning Family Roles and Rules

All groups create, learn, adopt, enact, replay, remake, and discard various kinds of roles and develop systems of rules to manage them. Roles are useful as they can help guide behavior (just follow the rules of the role!), but roles can also restrict behaviors and limit spontaneity and creativity. It is in the family unit where we first learn and play roles. Most family communication textbooks include chapters on family roles and rules. In these texts we can learn about adults' roles, but in order to have a complete understanding of family life, we also need to understand children's roles as well as how family roles and rules, inside and outside of home, are learned. So, in this chapter we will focus on family roles and rules from the point of view of children. Specifically, we will (1) define the concepts of family roles and rules and review related research in light of children, (2) describe the processes of children learning family roles and rules, and (3) suggest ways that families can use communication to facilitate positive role and rule development in the service of orchestrating and directing the development of children's potentialities.

Family Roles and Children

A **role** can be generally defined as a set of expected behaviors, or a framework of instructions that guide individuals as they enact or play a given role. Within families there are many roles children play. Some children's family roles are formal (created by societal agreements) such as son, daughter, brother, sister, stepchild, foster child, and so on. Some are informal (the unique creations of families), such as the goofy child, the jock, the brain, and so on. In Tom's family, for example, his father once cast him in the informal role of "speaker of the house" and calls upon him to give toasts and eulogies at family gatherings. His great uncle, an Iowa farmer, cast him in the informal role of "professor" (after he and lifelong friend John Dee had won a science fair at age 12), and Toms' brothers as the "agitator" and the "senator." Interestingly, the "agitator" (Mike) became a noted social worker who developed supported employment programs and championed the rights of developmentally disabled young adults (until he passed away at age 40). The "senator" later became a manager of information systems in healthcare where he uses his political and negotiation skills, and of course, Tom became a professor.

Theoretical models categorize family roles according to their functions. For example, the McMaster Model of Family Functioning (Epstein, Bishop, & Baldwin, 1982) includes five family functions that underlie family roles: adult sexual fulfillment and gender modeling for children, nurturance and emotional support, support of individual development, kinship maintenance and family management, and provision of basic resources. Although children are mentioned as an audience for gender modeling, the McMaster Model and others like it emphasize adult-centered functions, leave out child-specific roles, and say little about family role development processes, tacitly assuming that children will somehow learn to play adult family roles.

When children have been included in scholarly discussions of family roles, the focus has been on roles thrust upon them by birth order, age, or year in school; gender roles; and children's family roles that develop in response to family dysfunction and/or parental or family qualities.

Birth Order and Age-Related Roles

Some models of children's family roles focus on children's position in order of birth. Are you the "oldest child" in your family?

If so, have you noticed differences in how your younger siblings were treated by your parents? Are you among the youngest in your family? Have your parents treated you differently than older siblings? If you are a middle child, do you feel lost in the pack or squeezed between older and younger siblings? How do you feel about being the oldest or the youngest? How do your siblings feel about you? Julie is second of five, escaping the worst of the eldest's duties, but she did have some responsibilities for younger siblings nonetheless. In large families, the step-down effect is pretty common. On the other hand, the spotlight was not on her as brightly as on her older sister, so she felt free to date at a younger age! Tom is the oldest of three brothers and remembers his parents saying that more was expected of him and because he was a first-born, he was expected to set a good example for his brothers, and to watch out for them.

Early theory and research. Early research on birth order was prompted by the psychoanalytic theorizing of Alfred Adler (1956), a contemporary of Freud. Adler theorized that birth order had profound and lasting effects on the development of personality, and that middle children would be most likely to develop into successful individuals. According to Adler, eldest children had to work extra hard to regain lost parental attention to new siblings, and youngest children were overindulged by parents and lacked empathy. Although Adler's theory might be cheered by middle-borns, resonate with first-borns, and be somewhat rejected by later-borns, Adler offered no evidence to support his theory. Subsequent research, however, did find evidence to support weaker forms of Adler's claim.

Birth position, among many variables, can exert a moderate effect on the development of personality traits (openness, conscientiousness, extroversion, agreeableness, and neuroticism). First-borns have been found to tend towards greater openness, conscientiousness, and extroversion; less agreeableness and openness to new ideas than later-borns (Sulloway, 2001). And, young adults' self-perceptions of roles were found to correlate with actual birth order. Pulakos (1987), for example, found that in families of at least three children, first-borns perceived themselves to play a "responsible" role, middle-borns "popular and socially ambitious" roles, followed by youngest children "over-privileged" roles (Pulakos, 1987). It is important to remember, however, that *perceiving* a role (whether self-perception or a perception of others) is not necessarily the same as actually *enacting* a role. Another weakness is that birth-order research sheds little light on two-children and single-child families.

It makes sense that children of varied birth positions encounter different kinds of family social circumstances and experience different family role expectations. Parents of first-borns do not have to divide their time among other children as they must with later-borns. This affords first-borns more experience communicating with adults than later-borns. And in families with multiple children, first-borns often play the role of "parental helper" with their younger siblings. This can deepen and expand their communication learning as a result of playing the helper role – a good way to really learn something is to teach what you know to someone else. For example, while babysitting younger siblings, older siblings can practice parenting skills.

Siblings. The presence of siblings does affect children's role development in various ways: (a) first-borns may spend more time interacting in vertical (authority) relationships with adults than later-borns, (b) later-borns and first-borns both benefit by having to adapt to each other's different levels of communication skills and experience thereby gaining skill in horizontal relationships (with peers) (Mannle & Tomasello, 1987), (c) parents' perceptions of birth order can affect children's role development, and (d) the complexity of roles in parent–child relationships increases in families with multiple children. Dunn and Kendrick (1982), for example, found that qualities of mother–child role relationships at the birth of a second child affected siblings' role relationships one year later, such that qualities in the mother–first born relationship were also found later in the siblings' relationships. This means that caregivers need to give extra thought to communication with their first-borns as this interaction forms a pattern that will carry over to later-borns.

Parents. When thinking about children's birth-order roles and family communication, it is important also to consider that parents too are developing in their roles along with their children. Parents-of-first-borns are relatively inexperienced at childrearing and may rely heavily on their childhood recollections of their parents' behaviors, advice from family members (especially mothers), and media (baby books, parenting magazines, websites, etc.) as they enact new parent roles. Parents-of-subsequent-children, who are more experienced at communicating with children, may rely more heavily on their own experiences with their first-born as a guide to how to enact the parental role rather than on childhood memories, advice from family members, and media.

Assumptions. Let's look a bit more closely at the assumption behind the birth-order prediction. Across huge data sets, a correlation has been found between low IQ and later-born position in large families. But which comes first, the large family or low IQ? When measured within families, rather than across, the effect disappears (Rodgers, Cleveland, van den Ooord, & Rowe, 2000). Rogers and his colleagues suggest that although low-IQ parents may make larger families, the reverse does not hold. What does make the difference? Parenting behaviors do seem to change with birth order. Parents report higher expectations for first-borns than for later-borns (Baskett, 1984). First-borns themselves reported an authoritarian parent and tended more to introversion and judgment than did later-borns. Later-borns scored higher on extroversion and perceiving, and reported a combination of parenting styles (Stansbury & Coll, 1998). As Julie's mother answers the question of why she was harder on the older kids, "You just get tired and let the younger ones get away with more."

Siblings are very different people, growing up in the same family. What makes the differences among them? Dunn (1991) proposes several factors beyond birth position that contribute to nonshared experiences: the consistency of parenting to each child at each age (Is mother likely to treat the oldest child at 2 the same as the youngest at 2?); the stability of behavior with each child over time (Does mother comfort the distressed child to the same extent at age 2, at age 8, at age 16?); and the attention that children pay to interaction among other family members (Will the youngest have the richest interaction to observe? Will the oldest have the best, most attentive, adult models?) That is, the family communication each child has the opportunity to observe is likely to be at least somewhat unique to that child, with unique outcomes.

Children do notice parental differential treatment, and will respond to it in whatever way is available to them – direct complaints, indirect behavior, or silent internalization. Authoritative parents are more likely to accept direct complaints; authoritarian parents will never hear about the child's observation that parents play favorites, but their children's indirect messages may be more problematic. In preschool, when children have fewer and simpler spoken communication skills, more conflict and hostility has been observed among siblings whose parents treat them differentially (Dunn, 1988). However, siblings in middle childhood who perceive differential treatment also demonstrate more conflict and hostility (Brody, Stoneman, & Burke, 1987). Either few parents of multiple children invite direct complaints, or most siblings take out their frustrations on each other rather than on the parents who treat them differentially, or both.

Parents, whether they are aware of it or not, typically do have favorites at some time during siblings' childhoods. Among mothers who thought they treated their children similarly, researchers observed differential treatment with differential effects. In particular, when mothers showed greater affection to a younger sibling, the older sibling's perspective-taking ability improved. Indeed, the greater the difference in affection demonstrated to the two siblings, the better the older sibling was at assessing others' feelings and motives (Dunn & Munn, 1985, 1986, 1987). Not only did the older child learn to read mother's feelings well, the realization that the bulk of her affection was for the younger child led to lower self-esteem in the older (Dunn, 1991, p. 120).

Effects on communication. So, in terms of communication, an older child who observes the younger family member receive the lion's share of affection and attention may suffer lower self-esteem, but learns a great deal about how to read people's emotions. On the other hand, the younger child gains spoken-language facility by hearing the more complex speech mother is likely to direct to an older child. One group of scholars (Oshima-Takane, Goodz, & Derevensky, 1996) chose personal pronouns to observe in second-borns, because they are advanced linguistic forms requiring reversal for appropriate use (e.g. *you* becomes *me* in the back and forth of conversation) and because toddlers have few opportunities to observe the use of second-person pronouns in the speech directed to them. Indeed, second-borns were more advanced in personal pronoun production, having observed how to distinguish those pronouns accurately in their use between mother and the older sibling (e.g. "Hand me *my* keys and I'll get *your* jacket from the car.")

Chronological age. Age and grade-in-school have also been used to define children's roles at home and outside the family. Infant, toddler, preschooler, grader-schooler, middle-schooler, tween, teen, high-schooler, young adult, and adult–child (18 to 21+ years) are common labels for children's roles that can be used by communicators to orient to each other. Pre-linguistic infants of course do not know they are playing the role of "infant," but as we read in an earlier chapter, psychologist Jerome Bruner has shown that parents do treat their infants as if they were participants in interaction – "Where's my good little Cowboy?" "How's my princess doing today?" Older age-specific roles, such as "preschooler," are useful for adults as they orient themselves to communicating with a child. Children are less knowledgeable and less experienced communicators, and may not understand their own abilities, so it is important for adults to understand the child's age-specific role abilities to facilitate interaction as well as to **scaffold** or structure interaction to maximize a child's learning. For example, between ages 3 and 5, preschoolers are building on basic understandings of others as unique communicators and trying out a wide variety of new speech acts (demands, jokes, teases, etc., see Haslett & Samter, 1997, ch. 4). Understanding the communication behaviors typical of the preschooler role benefits adult communicators by helping them orient their messages to the child as well as to help the child work on speech acts and so on. From the child's point of view, caregivers' messages become the first bricks in the foundation of later role play and development. Childhood is a time to pretend, try out, and experiment with roles (familiar, societal, work, etc.) that may later either become a core part of identity or remain on the periphery of self.

Meanings of age-related labels for children's roles are also historically dependent and created for various social and cultural reasons. For example, due in part to harsh economic circumstances, in the Middle Ages the label "children" referred to small-scale adults of little value until they could assume the role of "worker" (at ages 7 to 12!) (Heywood, 2001). Today, in spite of global financial crises, economic circumstances are relatively better in some countries and **childhood** typically refers to a prolonged period of development characterized by relative protection from the adult world (e.g. adult topics, adult stresses, adult media content, etc.). To be sure, raising children over this long period of time is expensive (to calculate the costs of raising a child to age 18 in the US see the United States Department of Agriculture (2009); and for those in the UK see the Financial Services Authority (2009)). But, as much as some parents may joke about wanting to send their children off to work, today's legal and ethical culture, including child labor laws, prevent a return to the Middle Ages.

Sometimes age-specific terms for children have little to do with positive child development. The contemporary term, "tween," for example, refers to pre-adolescents ages 9 to 14 and was coined by marketers to create a new market segment for the direct sale of goods and services as well as to enlist the help of tweens to sell goods and services to parents (Levasseur, 2007). Although they do not yet have jobs (though they may be given allowances), tweens watch lots of television and use computers extensively where they are exposed to advertising intended to create demand for tween products (e.g. video games, sugared foods, etc.), develop brand identity and brand loyalty, as well as influence the buying habits of their parents in areas such as food purchases, vacationing, and more. The role of "consumer" is being shaped by forces outside the home as well as from within as is the case with gender roles.

Gender Roles

Sets of expected behaviors organized according to masculinity-femininity are called **gender roles** and the process of learning gender roles is referred to as **gender role socialization**. All roles are social constructions, or the products of agreements reached in interactions. And, as social constructions, they are open to interpretation and re-creation. Returning to the Middle Ages for another moment, we find the example of mothers teaching girls as young as 12 to be wives and mothers, including instruction in how to "spin, sew . . . manage a household, and . . . virtues of humility and submissiveness" (Heywood, 2001, p. 105). Similarly, boys in the Middle Ages were prepared by their fathers for military life, horse-riding, hunting, hawking, and some were given religious instruction and formal schooling. Preparing for fatherhood was not a prominent feature of boys' gender role socialization in the Middle Ages. Today, weaker forms of historical gender roles continue in many US families, and stronger forms are found in Middle Eastern and Asian cultures. In heterosexual families male and female children continue to receive different kinds of messages from their parents, experience different parental expectations, receive sex-typed toys, and are assigned different household jobs (Turner & West, 2002). In gay/lesbian households, gender role socialization is characterized by greater freedom of choice in gender expression, an emphasis on equal responsibilities and individuality – in essence, not assigning sex-typed household jobs. Whether in harmony with or in rebellion of gender roles, gender influences children's socialization into family roles.

What were your favorite toys as a child? Did you have specific jobs as a daughter or son? Was it OK for the boys to roughhouse, but girls were expected to play "nicely?" Did mom and dad talk about some topics (such as sex) differently to you and your siblings? Did mom and dad suggest different kinds of careers for you and your siblings?

Today, in spite of the effect of gender roles, you might find it surprising to learn that researchers have concluded that there are actually few empirical differences in the communication of men and women (Canary & Hause, 1993); men and women can indeed be equally effective communicators. Although developmentally, girls do lead in early communication development, both boys and girls can eventually develop equally effective communication skills.

Children's Roles in Response to Family Dysfunction and Family Qualities

The above discussion of children's family roles assumes family circumstances considered to be normal or functional (without pathologies). However, children's roles in families experiencing dysfunction seem to be different. Wegscheider (1981), for example, found that children of alcoholic parents adopt one of four dysfunctional roles: hero (a child who is a helper, pleaser), scapegoat (a child who opposes family norms and is blamed for parents' problems), lost child (a child who withdraws and avoids family interaction), or mascot (a child who diffuses tensions by clowning and using humor). These dysfunctional roles are created and enacted by children as a way to cope with the instabilities, uncertainties, and negative interactions with alcohol-dependent parents. In therapeutic settings and support organizations, counselors will work to help children create more functional coping roles.

Children in troubled or stressed families sometimes cross adult/ child role boundaries to play roles of "little parents," a process labeled **parentification** (Byng-Hall, 2008). As mentioned earlier, older children can gain competence in a wide variety of skills by helping parents care for younger siblings, but playing parental roles extensively can have negative results for children such as lowered self-esteem, depression, and more (Byng-Hall, 2002).

Finally, sometimes children's roles in families are defined indirectly by their parents' roles, for example: children of immigrant or refugee parents (Segel & Mayadas, 2005), children of a particular ethnic cultural group (e.g. Socha & Diggs, 1999), or children of divorce. And sometimes children's family roles are defined via the legal system: adopted child, foster child, or ward of the state.

All of these roles are defined in response to a circumstance or a quality of the parents or family in which the child resides and can be useful in understanding children's roles in their home lives. However, care should be taken to avoid stereotyping children using these role categories – children occupy many family roles, in many ways, in many kinds of families.

Family Rules and Children

As children assume and enact family roles, they are doing so within a system of **rules** or followable prescriptions for what behaviors are obligated, preferred, or prohibited in social situations (Shimanoff, 1980). Playing the role of "joker" in a family, for example, involves not only understanding and enacting generally expected behaviors of a joker, but also understanding the family's systems of rules in which enacting joking can occur. What behaviors are OK for jokers to enact in a particular family? What behaviors might be inappropriate? What behaviors are jokers prohibited from enacting? In the comedy film, *Raw*, for example, there is a scene where a young actor playing the comedian Eddie Murphy as a child entertains his relatives at a family gathering using various humor strategies generally considered to be antisocial, gross, scatological, and so on. Some of the relatives laugh, while others do not seem entertained. How would your household respond to these kinds of messages? Who would laugh? Who would not? Their responses and whether such messages occur at all depend in part on family rules. But, before turning our attention to children and family communication rules, let's first consider that family roles and rules are part of a larger umbrella of family governance.

Family Governance

All social systems, including families, develop a system of **family governance**, structures of interaction where leaders and followers set goals, endorse values, make policies, develop procedures, and direct the behaviors of members. In family governance, it is commonplace that adult members function in the role of "family leaders" and minor-children serve as "family followers." Indeed, in most societies adult family members are responsible, and usually held legally liable, for the wellbeing and behaviors of their minor children both inside and outside of home until their children reach the age of majority (e.g. age 18 in the US). As **open systems** – systems with boundaries that are permeable or open to the outside world – family governance is shaped by societal forces as well as forces inside families. For example, a virtue such as bravery is valued in many societies, but the extent to which a society's members are brave depends in part on the extent to which families adopt and teach the virtue of bravery to their children. There is a degree of truth in the expression – the hand that rocks the cradle rules the world.

However, it is important to understand that **power** or "the ability to act or affect [someone or something]" (*Oxford English Dictionary*, 2009) is an interactive quality of adults and children. The actions of adults and children are mutually influential affecting family relationships, family systems, and potentially societal systems. Although they are often cast in the roles of family followers, children function as partners with their parents in family governance. They do not just follow, but actively participate to shape a family system's rules. If you have seen a parent scurrying out of a store attempting to console an unhappy child with a lollypop, then you have seen an example of a child participating in family governance (a minor rebellion). Children are also future family-leaders-in-training who, as adults, will participate in the governance of family life as well as society – children's hands rock future cradles.

One classic conceptual model of power (French & Raven, 1959) highlights three facets of power: power bases, power processes, and power outcomes. Society gives adults a kind of **power base** or a resource that can be used in power interactions called authority (or legitimate power): an agreement that gives adults the rights and responsibilities of leading family systems. Adults are charged with setting goals, shaping values, as well as setting and enforcing policies and procedures for minor family members. Although the role of the child in family governance has traditionally been set as the family follower who has little or no formal say in family goals, values, policies, and procedures, the child does wield considerable power within the family system and can affect decision-making, problem-solving, and conflict-management. Other power bases family members use include reward power, punishment power, referent power (e.g. being a role model, charming) and expert power (knowledgeable).

Power processes refer to using power in interactions. For example, a parent who compliments a child for displaying polite behavior during dinner is using reward power whereas a parent who scolds a child for displaying impolite behavior is using coercive or punishment power. A parent, who instructs a child as to what constitutes polite behavior and impolite behavior and why politeness is preferred, is using expert power.

Power outcomes are the results of power interactions and include decisions, solutions, new rules or procedures, as well as emotional outcomes like how participants feel about decisions, solutions, or rules, as well as themselves and each other. After instructing a child about the rules of polite behavior, is thinking about politeness in positive ways encouraged? Does the child want to try politeness? Is the communication climate such as that the child wants to keep trying politeness? A positive approach stresses creating family communication climates where children, as partners in family governance, can learn about power in ways that will serve them positively in the future.

Family Role and Rule Development in Children

Marcia Dixson (1995) developed a model of parent–child communication that is particularly useful to frame our discussion of children's learning family roles and rules. Her model contains four propositions. First, children's sets of beliefs and expectations about relationships (models of relationships) are shaped by communication with parents and caregivers. As parents and children engage in communication, they are not just sharing words and messages; they are sharing understandings about their relationship with each other and creating a context for how these messages are to be understood. For example, in raising their two children, Stephanie and Paul, Tom and his wife, Diana, encouraged them to engage in argument – advance claims using evidence or good reasons. So, when their children wanted to purchase something special for themselves, for example, they had to give at least three good reasons why. This practice of arguing was made age-appropriate by allowing all kinds of reasons to count early on, with a gradual increasing of the sophistication as to what counted as a good reason ("I like it" was an OK reason at age 5, but not at age 10). The practice of giving "three good reasons" was intended to teach their children that thinking, arguing, and debating is, in a civil society, how communicators reach agreements and under-standings; how the work of society gets done outside the home. Today as high-school students, both Stephanie and Paul under-stand and use debate at home, in school, and with their friends, and especially with dad as they continue to argue to try to get all kinds of expensive stuff!

Dixons' second proposition states that the child's model of rela-tionship, developed through interaction with parents, might not work in relationships children encounter beyond the family. This would prompt the child to revise their model or abandon it, and replace it with a new one. Taking arguing as an example of one relational skill, there might be occasions in school where arguing a point is not encouraged, or may be perceived as an attempt to grab power. Does the child stop all arguing, or revise the model of relational arguing?

Dixons' third and fourth propositions bring her model full circle when she proposes that parents and children influence each other, and that children's revised and new models are brought back into interaction with parents which in turn can prompt parents to change their models of interaction with their children and so on. Thus, as children interact with parents they are mutually shaping each other's models of roles and rules in dynamic and ongoing ways.

Family communication scholars Lynn Turner and Richard West

(2002) add an important point concerning family role development: family members can be called upon to enact various roles at various times during the course of family life, and these roles shift and change among family members. Providing children with role experience as caregivers of younger children or pets, for instance, builds a foundation for later assumption of caregiving roles at home when an ill parent might require the support of children as caregivers.

Social learning theory (Bandura, 1977) provides part of the framework, implicit in Dixson's model, for explaining how children learn roles and rules. First, who are children's role models? Tom's first academic conference paper, written with his close friend David Dawes in 1982, found that fictional superheroes figured large as role models for young children, whereas known adults like parents figured larger as role models for college students. This makes sense in that children spend lots of time with attractive fictional characters who are sensationalized and made larger than life by media. But of course, when college students face real-world interactions and obstacles, mom and dad start to look pretty good as role models. Short on rent money? College students wonder to themselves what dad and mom would do rather than Superman.

In terms of learning family rules, Socha (2006) focused on the topic of discipline, arguing that teaching children rules of behavior using primarily coercive power was limiting and in the long run less successful than using discussion. Children, he argued, have many potentialities to be discovered. Coaches of young T-ball players, for example, do not know if they are coaching a future major league player or a recreational player. As they watch children play, they notice their many mistakes and then go about correcting them, often loudly. Socha argued that children are supposed to make mistakes whether learning to play baseball, or communicate, and that it is up to caregivers and coaches to orchestrate circumstances in order to keep children wanting to participate, mistakes and all; that is, to positively direct children's behaviors towards desired goals and to expand the zone of proximal development. To illustrate this he used a common mishap – spilling milk at the table. A spill is a dining error that disrupts a meal, can ruin food, prompt bad feelings, and so on. All diners have the potential to spill. When a spill happens to a child, it is a dining mistake that could occur for many reasons. A negative approach to the spill would be to yell about the spill, speak negatively about the spiller, as well as sanction the spiller for the rule violation. However this approach fails to recognize that dining mistakes happen to all of us, that when we make a dining mistake we need strategies to correct the mistake and to manage the spoiled scene as well as the images of participants and the relationships in the scene. Socha suggests instead, that adults, as orchestrators and directors of children's potentialities should view spilled milk as a chance to teach children about handling dining errors by orchestrating children's meals to minimize spills (e.g. use of covered cups, seating diners farther apart, teaching them about controlled gestures) and when spills do occur then to direct children how to properly handle the dining error. Also, children should be praised when they execute a meal without dining errors – something often forgotten by parents. This approach motivates children to want to learn and to continue to develop their dining skills so that one day they may be skilled enough to enjoy the cuisine of a five-star restaurant.

Rules are essential tools to help guide us through communication episodes, and it is important to remember to help children navigate the many new rules and communication episodes they encounter at home and beyond.

Positive Family Communication Roles/Rules and Children

Today's families are complex and can include children living in multiple residences, in many kinds of family circumstances, and learning about roles and rules from a variety of caregivers of varying generations both inside and outside of home (Socha & Stamp, 2009). And, this complexity makes it difficult to fully describe the communication worlds of today's children. One model that has potential for describing this complexity is called the Convoy Model (Antonucci, 2001; Kahn & Antonucci, 1980) in which individuals are members of dynamic networks (convoys) that over the life course surround and support them as they encounter life experiences. Convoys are shaped by personal (age, gender, etc.) and situational (role expectations, resources, etc.) factors and provide a base from which individuals can draw resources to address life's obstacles as well as facilitate wellbeing as individuals grow. Although research on the convoy model is emerging, it makes sense to begin to think about the kinds of convoys that can best support children's learning and development. Of course, thinking about children's convoys will mean having to recognize that families sometimes might not possess all the necessary resources for optimal child development and that other social contexts might be needed. But, the model does help to describe the complexity of the role and rule systems in which today's children live and the need for effective communication among convoy participants.

Positive psychologist Mihaly Csikszentmihalyi (pronounced: Me-high Cheeks-sent-me-high) and colleagues (Csikszentmihalyi, Rathunde, & Whalen, 1997) studied talented teenagers including the roles played by families in their development. "Optimal conditions for teenage development (and it could be argued adult development as well) are not very different from what is necessary for nurturing infants . . . Just as infants need continuing security and support for the emergence of exploration and independence, so do all persons, no matter their age" (p. 154). The development of young children into talented teens requires families that are complex, encouraging *both* integration (stable connections between members) *and* differentiation (support for members' individuality in seeking out new challenges), thereby creating optimal environments for the blossoming of children's talents. Thus, to support the development of talent, families need sensible rules to help structure family and children's time, and family roles that encourage children to do their best: provide both high support and high challenge.

In the next chapter we will focus on the important processes of making choices, solving problems and handling conflicts that occur in the everyday lives of children in families.

Activities

1. What does "childhood" mean to you? When should a person be considered an "adult?" Write your own definitions for the terms "child" and "adult."
2. What kinds of roles did you play in your family as a child? Think about the roles that you play today. Are their similarities? Differences? Why? How did your early roles influence your current roles?
3. Make a list of the kinds of qualities you think an ideal boss, ideal teacher, and ideal parent should possess. What items are common in your three lists? Unique to a particular role?
4. Think about the kinds of toys, books, and television shows you engaged with as a child and their influence in teaching you about gender roles. Who were your TV heroes/heroines? Who were your favorite characters in books? What were your favorite toys? Will you share your favorite toys and books with your sons and daughters?
5. Think of a talent that you have. What kinds of family rules and roles facilitated development of this talent? Inhibited the development of this talent?

Suggested Further Reading

Csikszentmihalyi, M., Rathunde, K., & Whalen, S. (1997). *Talented teenagers: The roots of success & failure*. Cambridge, UK: Cambridge University Press.

Dixson, M. (1995). Models and perspective of parent–child communication. In T. J. Socha & G. H. Stamp (eds), *Parents, children and communication: Frontiers of theory and research* (pp. 43–61). Mahwah, NJ: Lawrence Erlbaum.

Haslett, B. B., & Samter, W. (1997). *Children communicating: The first five years*. [ch. 6: Family influences on communicative and social development.] Mahwah, NJ: Lawrence Erlbaum.

Heywood, C. (2001). *A history of childhood*. Cambridge, UK: Polity.

5

Children in Family Decisions, Problems, and Conflicts

Families face an incredible array of alternatives in everyday life and making choices among alternatives is the process of **decision-making**. Some decisions are left to individual family members. What to eat, what to wear (or not), style of hair and more are choices that are shaped mostly by personal preferences, individual values, identity, mood, and so on. Some decisions are shared or **conjoint decisions**. Taking family vacations, celebrating holidays, having additional children, and more, depend on shared and agreed upon family preferences, family values, family identity, family climate, and so on. As you read in the previous chapter, one consequence of children interacting with family members is the development of family rules and roles that guide and shape family communication. Of course, family rules and roles also affect choices. Is a decision left to a particular individual? Or, is it to be shared? Does a family follow traditional gender roles and assign decisions about a home's exterior maintenance, for example, to an adult male and decisions about a home's interior maintenance to an adult female? Or, are a family's roles non-gender-specific where all adult family members have an equal say in decisions about matters outside and inside the home? Are children involved in making family choices? If so, which ones? How much say do children have? As with all communication processes, families communicating about decisions set up an important context in which children learn about communication and decision-making. Of course decisions, rules, as family participants all change with time and require adjustment.

100

In everyday life families also encounter **problems** or situations where alternatives are either unknown or not completely clear. Some problems are unexpected and prompt crises: medical diagnoses of major or terminal illness, job loss, and so on, while other problems may be expected to occur as a part of the natural course of human development: an increasing need for daily living assistance by elderly family members, economic needs of growing children (saving for college!), and more.

Families face many kinds of problems. Some problems are **life-threatening**; disease, homelessness, malnutrition, violence, and war threaten the survival of far too many children and families (see UNICEF, 2009). Although not necessarily life-threatening, **major problems** pose significant risks to the health and well-being of children and families and can become life-threatening. Acute and chronic illness (mental, physical), cruelty (physical, emotional, verbal abuse, etc.), crime/incarceration, disabilities (developmental, educational, physical, etc.), divorce, substance abuse, unemployment, and more, are among major problems that can deplete family resources and impair families' abilities to provide for the health and wellbeing of their members.

Beyond life-threatening and major problems, children and families also experience a wide array of **minor problems** that pose relatively smaller risks to the health and wellbeing of children and families and create minor obstacles to optimal development. Children lacking support for homework assignments, minor physical injuries, transportation problems (flat tires, etc.), not getting invited to particular parties, and many more are commonplace minor problems. Both major problems and minor problems can also occur with some regularity (**chronic problems**) and minor chronic problems can sometimes evolve into major problems (e.g. the child who is not invited to social occasions may become isolated and depressed).

Problems are inevitable; a reality of everyday life. We cannot not encounter problems, of some degree and kind, during our lives. Most family communication texts have lots to say about problems, crises, and the stress of problems on families. In this text we advocate for a positive approach and urge families to develop their capacities and strengths so that they might optimally manage and cope with inevitable problems. **Resiliency** is "characterized by patterns of positive adaptation in the context of significant adversity or risk" (Masten & Reed, 2002, p. 75), or in general terms, resiliency is the capacity to cope with life's ongoing problems. Resilient children and families develop ways to think about problems and to manage problems that help them to thrive in spite of life's obstacles. Resilient family members and children develop capacities (creativity, and more) that might help to prevent some problems as well as aid in their management.

As families face decisions and problems, they can also experience contrasting communication-styles, varied opinions, disagreements about facts, clashes over values, divergent policies, scarce resources, or, in more general terms, **conflict**. Like decisions and problems, conflicts are an inevitable, inherent aspect of everyday family life, and resilient families are those that effectively manage conflicts. For children, learning and practicing effective conflict management skills is especially important, as research has shown that their future mental and physical wellbeing as adult married persons depends in part on their use of positive conflict styles such as positive problem-solving (Gottman, 1994; Segrin, Hanzel, & Domschke, 2009). On the dark side, physically abusive behaviors have a greater chance of occurring after failed attempts to verbally manage episodes of conflict (Wilson et al., 2006).

In this chapter we focus on the role of family communication in increasing children's resiliency by examining family communication in making decisions, managing problems, and handling conflicts. In particular, we take a closer look at children's roles in these family areas, as well as developmental communication implications in each area. We continue to emphasize a positive approach that features using communication to prompt positive emotions and positive cognitions such as hope and optimism, and propose to increase children's resiliency by means of positive family communication related to making good choices, effectively managing problems, and successfully navigating conflicts.

Decision-Making

Individual Decision-Making

Let's start with an overview of the psychology of individuals making decisions, consider the role of communication in making individual decisions, and then discuss how families might use communication to facilitate the positive development of these processes. We will then examine the process of making decisions with more than one family member (conjoint decision-making) as well as the role that families play in teaching children about group communication and decision-making.

Making a decision involves choosing from among alternatives. A **choice** is an expression of preference, that is, when choosing one kind of soft drink rather than another, at that moment, one is communicating that this particular soft drink is somehow valued or preferred. The psychology of individual decision-making tries to explain how choices are made as well as why we choose as we do.

We all want to make "good choices" and of course parents want their children to make "good choices." Parents and caregivers convey messages to help children to learn to make good choices. But what makes a choice "good" or "better" than another? How does a decision-maker know that a particular choice will in fact be "good"?

Psychologists have developed various models of individual decision-making. Let's examine two of them, Subjective Expected Utility Theory (SEUT) (Savage, 1954) and Prospect Theory (Kahneman & Tversky, 1979), before we consider the role of communication making individual decisions.

According to SEUT, individuals make choices using personal judgments of **expected values** and personal analyses of the **subjective probabilities** of the occurrence of each outcome. That is, when faced with alternatives, a decision-maker is thought to examine each option to determine its expected value (rewards less costs) as well as guess what the odds are that these good and bad things will happen if the option is chosen (its subjective probability). Let's say a 7-year-old boy is at a skateboard store with his generous uncle who promised to buy him any skateboard he wanted (i.e. money is no object). Which skateboard should he choose? According to SEUT, the boy would estimate the benefits and costs of each skateboard as well as guess the chances that these pluses (less the minuses) will occur. The skateboard he chooses will be the one that maximizes his personal judgments of subjective expected utility. Notice that SEUT assumes: (a) the boy will approach the choice rationally (ground his choice in logic), and (b) the boy has all the available information about all of these skateboards.

It is of course theoretically possible that 7-year-old boys might approach a skateboard choice very rationally and also be very knowledgeable about skateboards (maybe more so than his uncle and parents). However, in practice as well as in theory, it is unrealistic to expect that a young boy (or many of us) will actually take the time to carefully assess each and every possible skateboard, let alone know for sure the characteristics of each and every skateboard. It is more likely that the boy will employ a somewhat different process outlined in Prospect Theory (Kahneman & Tversky, 1979).

According to Prospect Theory, individuals use **heuristics**, shortcuts or rules of thumb, to help manage information when making choices. In making the skateboard choice, instead of conducting extensive research into each skateboard, the boy is likely to take shortcuts – use heuristics – to narrow his choices to those boards that, say, he has seen his friend riding and/or Tony Hawk, a professional skateboarder, endorsing. Of course, in choosing to use heuristics, the boy has let **biases** – unwanted and/or unintended influences – enter his choice-making; he is privileging information in his immediate environment over that which he could find in other contexts, such as libraries; as well as easily obtainable information over that which takes effort.

Prospect Theory also considers that we are each different in our personal reference points for making decisions and using heuristics. Children seem to prefer quick, easy choices, while adults may take more time and have learned to see choices in more complex terms, especially in situations of high risk. Some individuals generally avoid risk in making choices, others don't mind taking on some risk, while still others are risk seekers. Research shows that high risk and high sensation-seeking children who lack resistance competencies (abilities to say no) are likely to later on make maladaptive choices to use illegal drugs, engage in underage drinking, and so on (Hecht & Miller Day, 2009). Individuals can also change personal preference points as a function of a given decision. Decisions that involve greater risks, to monetary resources for example, can prompt caution.

According to Prospect Theory, decision-making involves two stages, first, individuals use heuristics to assess and order choices according to their personal reference point, and second, they evaluate the subjective probability of the occurrence of these alternatives. Thus, a person's choice can be explained in part by examining heuristics and biases used in the valuing of alternatives, personal reference points concerning information use, the extent of risk a person is willing to take, and so on. Like SEUT, Prospect Theory also assumes that a decision-maker is behaving rationally, but does acknowledge that taking shortcuts limits our chances of making optimal choices.

In sum, when facing a decision, individuals use: (a) available information about alternatives, (b) personal assessments of the value of the alternatives as well as the chances of these values happening, (c) heuristics to simplify information processing, which introduces biases into decision processes that potentially can reduce the chance of making a good choice as well as (d) personal reference points concerning information use and risk.

Family Communication and Individual Decision-Making

So how is communication connected to individual decision-making? It is through communication that we share and acquire information about alternatives as well as critica" information and develop the processes we use to ma (heuristics and biases). Messages can influence the alternatives and their respective probabilities as wel personal reference points. It is through communicat create decision-making procedures, and monitor the quality of decision-making processes and outcomes. And, especially for children, learning to make individual choices is an important part of the process of crafting their identities, discovering their likes/dislikes as well as their signature strengths. In this section we examine the sources of decision information, the development of decision-making communication, and an important factor that can inhibit the development of optimal decision-making.

Sources of decision information. As the boy and his uncle contemplate their skateboard purchase, let's say a salesperson talks about various boards. Framed in terms of individual decision-making, the salesperson's messages seek to increase the boy's valuation of the qualities of particular boards (likely the expensive ones) as well as assure the boy and his uncle that the boards will deliver these positive outcomes (e.g. "Tony Hawk rides this board, dude!"). To the extent the boy relies on a heuristic (using information that is immediately available, rather than executing an extensive research study), and values Tony Hawk's abilities, the boy will value that alternative more than the others. However, if the boy's uncle should add that he read in a skater magazine about a particular board's spotty durability record, and that other boards would likely prove more durable, then the boy must choose whom to believe: his uncle or the salesperson. As with all decision-makers, children must assess the credibility of information sources when sifting through available information relevant to a decision.

Many sources can affect decision-making, and for children some sources can be highly influential: parents, siblings, extended family, friends, peers, family professionals (family's physician, family's religious/spiritual leaders, teachers, coaches, etc.), commercial interests (advertisers, media conglomerates, etc.), and more. Due to children's extensive viewing of screened media (TV, DVD, Internet, etc.) commercial interests also exert considerable weight in shaping a wide array of children's decisions (Weintraub-Austin, Hust, & Kistler, 2009). For example, children in the primary grades who regularly viewed a daily TV commercial as a requirement of a school's participation in the Channel One rogram (where schools receive media equipment in exchange for viewing agreements) developed signs of brand identification and brand loyalty (Fox, 2000). Also viewing commercials increased the odds that children would include the qualities of a product in their personal descriptions of self (e.g. shapes of children's heads in self-portraits mirrored the shape of a character's head of a commercial they had viewed; Fox, 2000). In addition, marketers also directly enlist children's help to exert influence on their parents' decision-making (consumer, social, and political): a process labeled the "nag factor" or "pester power" (Weintraub-Austin, Hust, & Kistler, 2009, p. 217).

The process of adults assessing the credibility of a source has been studied by persuasion scholars since Aristotle. However, in part because adults often make children's choices for them, the role of family communication in shaping how children learn to make credibility judgments, and how children's credibility judgments affect their decision-making is unclear and requires further study. At this point, we do know that it is important to help children understand that when making a decision it is important to gather information from many sources and that sources should be trustworthy.

Development of individual decision-making and communication. Of course, parents and caregivers must make choices for infants. But, infants will also communicate to parents and caregivers when they do not prefer a particular choice – usually pretty loudly! However, as children's language, cognitive, and communicative abilities develop, opportunities also arise to facilitate the development of children's individual decision-making skills in age-appropriate ways. Parents will have many opportunities to help children recognize when to make decisions, talk about the merits of alternatives, teach children about heuristics and biases, help children learn about and come to understand their personal reference points, work with varied information sources, and so on.

Teaching children about individual decision-making is an ongoing, daily activity that forms important foundations for future decision-making. Let's look at an example of making an important, repetitive individual decision: choosing what to wear. Parents of young children (ages 3–5) are often in a hurry to get the kids to preschool and themselves to work, and so, often tell their child what to wear. However, parents mindful of teaching individual decision-making skills, can take a little time to create a scaffold for selecting clothing by laying out two outfits, talking with the child about which outfit might best fit the day's activities, and then giving the child a few moments to decide which outfit to choose. Why is it important to take the time to build this foundation? The process of choosing what to wear (or not to wear) is highly repetitive, yet very important. The popular US cable TV show, *What Not to Wear* (The Learning Channel) illustrates the many kinds of problems that can arise when decision-making about clothing is neglected for long periods of time, is based on faulty or unreliable information, and so on. Clothing choices are of course related to the expression of individual identity, as well as interlinked with economics, social structures (e.g. fitting in), and more. So by helping a child in age-appropriate ways to become mindful of clothing choices, to understand the consequences of clothing choices, to appreciate the values that motivate clothing choices, and so on, adults are providing an important decision-making skill that can later serve the child well when they are making personal choices as teens.

Daily, there are many decision points where parents and caregivers can present decisions to children and scaffold decision-making processes. It is understandable that some parents may be uncomfortable turning over individual decision-making power to young children and impatient with the time required talking about decisions. Yet parents and caregivers should remember that the foundation for individual decision-making is built in early inter-action and that children will build on that foundation to one day make good choices on their own! Given the many individual decisions in everyday life, lots of time could and should be devoted to talking about making choices.

Outside the family, children in the primary grades (1–3) are exposed to character-education programs that sometimes include decision-making. In general, these programs are intended to help build children's personal strengths and qualities. In particular, one character-education program specifically focuses on teaching children good decision-making skills: Lifegoals (Reynolds, 2005). The program's curriculum covers children in grades K-6 and uses a model of decision-making called Goal-Oriented Option Development (GOOD) that features: identifying choice options, discerning pluses and minuses and decision implications in the short term (consequences) and long term (outcomes), recognizing the goals for a decision, and understanding motivational forces behind choice-making. Communication skills figure large in the Lifegoals program as children read and role-play case studies and then employ the GOOD model to help them organize their choice-making. Although Lifegoals is intended for classroom use (and has undergone testing and assessment that support its validity; Reynolds, 2005), the general aims of the programs seem also translatable to everyday family life. For example, by talking-aloud individual decisions – as we all do in private speech for self about unfamiliar problems – family members can make transparent their individual decision-making processes and thus assist children in understanding how adults make choices. Also, enlisting the input of children in the process of adults' making individual choices may suggest alternatives to adults that might have gone unseen! As educational programs like Lifegoals have shown, it is the talking-aloud process through which children can be helped to learn how to make choices rather than passively observing and guessing what's going on. Talking-aloud capitalizes on the child's own way of figuring problems by way of egocentric and private speech.

An inhibiting factor – deferring gratification. Parents and caregivers, however, should be aware of developmental factors that work against effective decision-making, and be able to use their communication skills to manage these factors. One of the more prominent inhibiting factors working against effective individual decision-making is children's low impulse control, or desire for immediate gratification. The text below describes the Marshmallow Experiment that highlights the importance of helping young children (they focused on 4-year-olds but their findings can apply to us all) to resist the temptation to grab the first solution, product, or alternative offered.

109

The Marshmallow Experiment Revisited

Psychologist Walter Mishel conducted a now famous study from the 1960s, where an investigator leads a preschooler (age 4) into a room where there is a plate with one marshmallow on a table (in an updated version its four m & m candies). The investigator tells the child that if she/he does not eat the marshmallow/candy until the investigator returns then she/he will receive two marshmallows (or 8 m & m candies). The investigator leaves and returns 12–20 minutes later (during which time the children's behaviors are videotaped). Children who waited to eat the marshmallow/candy (deferred gratification) became better adjusted adolescents, who were more dependable, and scored higher on standardized achievement tests than those who immediately ate the marshmallow/candy (Mishel, Shoda, & Rodriguez, 1989). Why? Watching the children's behaviors provides a clue. Those children who delayed eating the marshmallow/candy worked very hard to distract themselves from the forbidden stimulus by singing, turning their backs on the marshmallow, talking to themselves, and more. The skills of identifying and keeping a goal in sight while avoiding distractions and temptations is a very important part of success in almost every aspect of life – just ask any college student seeking a university degree! Reaching important major goals takes time, and learning patience and persistence in the face of failure is an important part of learning to make effective decisions.

Deferring gratification is difficult for young children (ages 2–5) to learn. And, unfortunately, advertising makes the job of teaching children to wait, think critically about options, and make good choices, more difficult by creating a "buy it now!" culture. However, parents and caregivers can teach children to resist this impulse, and help them to identify important life goals, the pathways to achieving these goals, and the value of persistence in working towards these goals. Similar to the child trying to not eat the single marshmallow in order to achieve something greater, it is worthwhile for adults and children to pursue activities that promise deeper and longer-lasting gratification and to avoid being distracted by those seductive, fleeting moments of pleasure. But, what kinds of activities promise happiness?

Studies of artists, athletes and talented teens (Csikszentmihalyi, 1990, 1996; Csikszentmihalyi, Rathunde, Whalen, & Wong, 1997) suggest that adults should help children to discover what they do well – their **signature strengths** – and to encourage them to develop increasingly complex understandings and challenging experiences as they use these signature strengths. Since most of life's most rewarding goals are reached over the long-run (e.g. education, employment, happy long-term family relationships), parents who assist in setting long-range goals and encourage children to work toward them are helping build the foundation for effective future decision-making as well as happy lives.

Decision-making is not just an individual process; it is also shared with other family members in both interpersonal decision-making and group decision-making. Next, we focus on shared decisions and communication's role in making them.

Conjoint Decision-making

Making choices as a couple or a group involves processes that are somewhat similar to making individual decisions including identifying, understanding, and evaluating alternatives; increasing mindfulness of the potential outcomes of choices; and so on. However, sharing choices is far more complex as it involves coordinating multiple and shared viewpoints, weighing multiple opinions, managing power struggles, reconciling divergent points of view, and more. Group communication scholars have also recognized that group decision processes not only change and develop over the life of a group, but also these processes change for the individual over the course of participation in multiple groups (Frey & Barge, 1997).

As you read in Chapter 3, family interaction gives children initial opportunities to experience, participate, and learn about group communication. In this section we focus on conjoint decision-making processes at home, in particular, individual–social group dynamics, types of group decisions, and leadership.

Individual–social group dynamics. Communication scholars Frey and Barge (1997, ch. 2) conceptualize group communication as involving the management of dialectical tensions at the individual and group levels. These tensions are present across four stages: (1) entering, (2) encountering others, (3) engaging tasks, and (4) ending. Let's apply these to families.

In the first stage, entering, say when beginning a family yard landscaping project, *motivation* is a primary individual theme (Do I really want help?), while increasing *identification* with the family task is a primary group theme. (We should all want to be proud of our yard.) That is, when embarking on a family project individuals face dialectical tensions like: I want to participate, but I also don't want to participate. I want the family to do well, but only want to put in my fair share of effort and so on. For families, the dialectical challenge is to get members to agree on the goals of the project while respecting individual's rights and needs; to identify with the family but also to remain individuals, and so on.

In stage two when encountering other members as they embark on the yard landscaping project, individuals face tensions of *relating* (I like being with my family, but I also want to be with my friends), and at the group level tensions concern *connecting* (We need to be cohesive, but not too cohesive). In the third stage of engaging the yard landscaping task, individuals confront tensions of *contributing* (How will I fit it? Will I lead? Follow?), while groups face tensions of *working* (establishing procedures, allowing for spontaneity, balancing member satisfaction with group productivity, etc.). And, in the final stage when ending the project (or groups), individual tensions involve *disengaging* (This was really fun, I want stay and I am happy with what we have done and unhappy with what we have done, etc.) and group tensions involve *terminating* (How do we bring closure to the project and remain committed to future projects?)

Group and individual level tensions are an inherent part of family group processes and rather than working to remove them, group communication scholars argue that we need to accept and manage them. For example, at the individual level, children want to identify with their families and form individual identities *at the same time*. These kinds of tensions are always present but are especially noticeable in situations such as when a teen asks mom or dad to drop them off at a friend's home, but please do not come in to talk with their friends. Or when, a 2-year-old wrestles a spoon away from a parent who is feeding him/her saying, "I do it!" As families interact in everyday life as a unit, they can increase children's mindfulness about group and individual tensions and offer guidance about their management by talking about these tensions and reminding children that it is OK to struggle with these tensions.

Types of decisions. Families (as all groups) encounter three types of decisions: decisions of fact (Is something true or not? Did it occur or not?), decisions of value (Is something desirable or not?), and decisions of policy (Should something be done or not?). Families also develop criteria to determine the relative effectiveness of their choices (Is an answer to a factual decision the best possible? Does a choice best reflect the family values? Does a solution to a policy issue solve the problem?) Decisions of fact are necessary to making good policy and value decisions.

As families encounter decisions, they develop plans or structures to approach making choices in much the same way individuals make decisions. Decision plans include how to manage tasks associated with the decision (i.e. gathering information, assessing information, developing selection criteria as well as policies and procedures for these functions – who handles what, etc.) and the family relationships as it makes the decision (Is the family climate positive? Are family members motivated to work with each other? Arc thcy feeling positive about being a member of the family?)

Let's say that a family wants to plan a family vacation. This task involves management of many decisions of fact, value, and policy, as well as development of a decision plan as to how to approach the task. What do family members want from a vacation? Should they plan a staycation (vacationing at home)? Or go somewhere? What are their destination alternatives? How much will a given vacation choice cost? Should everyone's say weigh equally? Or, does dad have the final say? How will differing opinions be managed? What is known about the vacation destinations under consideration? Is a resort that was wonderful in an earlier family vacation, still likely to be OK (or was it damaged in a hurricane?) How much time can be devoted to the process of making this decision? How much research is the family willing to do? How will they communicate and use this information? As you can imagine (and have probably experienced), in order to cut down on all this decision labor, once families make a good choice (however that is defined), they tend to want to repeat it (Tom's family went to Wisconsin and Iowa, *a lot!*).

Fact, value, and policy decisions have functional requirements (task and relational) that need to be met if the family is to be successful in making decisions (Hirokawa & Salazar, 1997). In making a family vacation decision, does the family have enough factual information? Does it have information about alternatives? Does it have procedures to critically evaluate information? Does it have criteria to know when it has reached a decision (majority vote? unanimous?) Like individual decisions, family choices are also shaped by heuristics and biases that are shared among family members such as using information that is handy rather than gathered by research.

Children can learn much about communication and group decision-making processes in the context of family life, but unfortunately the extent to which families actually make decisions as a unit seems limited. More so, instead of making family decisions as a group, individual family members make de facto decisions (with little discussion), or decisions are made by policies that accommodate an individual or sub-group (sometimes with discussion). Sometimes families do make decision by consensus where members discuss and reach mutual agreements, although this is usually focused on adult members (see Galvin, Bylund, & Brommel, 2008, pp. 203–205). Socha and Socha (1994) found that young children's (ages 5–6) experiences with communication in decision-making groups outside of home (e.g., team sports, choirs, scouting) is also very limited, but that with some training children can learn to approximate the communication decision-making patterns of adult groups.

114

In spite of what seems to be limited opportunities to experience communication and group decision-making in the context of families, and although more research about children's communication in family decision-making is needed, the family remains an important context for children's initial exposure to these processes as well as a context in which there is much potential to learn about group communication and decision-making processes.

Leadership. Another important feature of group communication that children begin to learn in their families is leadership communication. Most studies of group leadership have examined group leader's communication style, connections between leaders' communication styles, the kinds of tasks leaders help a group to manage, and relationships between and among group members.

There are interesting parallels between styles of group leadership and styles of parenting. In the group communication literature we find three primary styles of group leading: autocratic (by edict), democratic (by discussion), and laissez faire (by emergence) (Lewin & Lippitt, 1938). In the family communication literature, we find three styles of parenting: authoritarian (Do it!), authoritative (Let's discuss it), and/or permissive (Let's see what happens) (Baumrind, 1971). Although studies of group leadership came well before studies of parenting, developmentally it makes sense that we find continuities between parenting styles and group leading styles since children are first exposed to parenting styles, followed by exposure to teacher's classroom management styles, and later group leadership styles of managers in the workplace. Thus, in households where authoritative parenting styles are the norm, children benefit from increased amounts of discussion and exposure to a prosocial style of leading that will benefit them as they participate in their future families and groups.

Summary

Children develop early decision-making skills in the context of family communication. By observing communication about decision-making at home, children are acquiring conceptual models they will carry forward into future episodes of decision-making. However, sometimes families face situations where the alternatives are not clear or are undesirable and this creates problems that require management.

Problem-Solving

In the course of everyday family life, **problems** – obstacles or impediments for which there are no immediate solutions – emerge that can inhibit families' growth and development, tax its resources, as well as prompt stress. Sometimes these problems are unpredictable (e.g., death, disability, divorce, illness, unexpected pregnancy) while others might be foreseen (e.g., future economic needs, needs of aging family members). Unlike decisions, problems do not come with a list of alternatives from which to choose the best one. There is usually no list at all. **Problem-solving** involves first identifying (often inventing) alternatives so that decision-making can proceed. Of course in spite of best efforts, unfortunately, sometimes no alternatives are desirable and a family must make the best possible choice from among undesirable alternatives and then manage the consequences of their choice. With many problems, alternatives must be invented, so following a positive approach, a key asset in developing effective problem-solving is creativity.

Creativity. Positive psychologist Csikszentmihalyi (1996) defines creativity as an interactive phenomenon: "**Creativity** is any act, idea, or product that changes an existing domain, or that transforms an existing domain into a new one . . . It is important to remember, however, that a domain cannot be changed without the explicit or implicit consent of a field responsible for it" (p. 28). That is, creativity is inherently social. If a person is unable to get others to adopt a new idea then the effort is best regarded as an attempt at creativity. Csikszentmihalyi et al. (1997, ch. 3) outlined ten attributes of creative individuals (in dialectical terms): having lots of energy and able to be at rest; smart and naïve; playful and disciplined; imaginative and grounded in reality; introverted and extroverted; humble and proud; masculine and feminine (free from gender role typing); rebellious and traditional; passionate and objective; open to suffering and open to enjoyment. Notice, many of these attributes could also be a part of the concept of "children" (often regarded as high in creativity).

Based on extensive study of artists, writers, painters, sculptors, and similar creative individuals, Csikszentmihalyi (1990) developed a theory to explain the intrinsic motivation of creativity called "Flow." The experience of being in flow refers to a state defined by: intense and focused concentration, a merging of action and awareness, a loss of a sense of self, a sense of control, distortion of time (losing track of), and experiencing the activity as intrinsically rewarding. Think of a child playing with building blocks, where the child is immersed in the activity, loses track of time, becomes one with the activity and loses his/her sense of self, and simply loves building with the blocks. Moments of flow result from achieving a balance between challenges and skills; too much challenge matched with too little skill prompts anxiety and too little challenge while having too much skill prompts boredom. Flow is a very desirable state that when experienced regularly correlates with a number of positive qualities including achievement, academic success, personal happiness and more. In what kinds of activities do you become happily lost? How about as a child? How about your parents? Your siblings?

Principles of flow have been used to redesign workplaces and museums, and at least one school created a "flow activities center" (Whalen, 1999) where children can pursue what is referred to as serious play. Csikszentmihalyi et al. (1997) has also examined the role of families in creating moments of flow and the development of talent. Based on a study of teenagers, he concluded: "optimal conditions for teenage development (and it could be argued for everyone's development) are not very different from what is necessary to nurture infants" and include "security and support for the emergence of exploration and independence" (p. 154). Families that encourage both integration (closeness) and differentiation (individual development), who encourage the play of dialectics, are called **complex families**. Complex families (relative to simple ones) create conditions optimal for the development of creativity and talent. They help their members to enjoy challenging activities that lead to achievements, use of talents, and personal happiness. Of course communication plays a significant role in creating conditions of flow as family members use messages that challenge each other to explore their talents, as well as support members as they use their talents. Complex family communication encourages creativity, exploration of new frontiers, helps members discover unrealized talents, and supports members as they seek to develop their talents. And although research is needed on this, it is our guess that complex families are probably effective at solving family problems.

Summary

Family problems do not come with a list of alternatives from which to choose, rather they are more like puzzles that require patience, time, and many efforts in order to develop workable solutions. From a positive perspective, creativity is an asset in family problem-solving, in that obstacles confronting families may have many possible ways around them, and it is up to families to develop innovative solutions for addressing problems. Creativity – experiencing moments of flow – is something that families can encourage by means of messages that challenge members to explore new horizons and undiscovered talents, as well as messages that support members to develop their signature strengths. However, as families make decisions and develop solutions to problems, it is inevitable that they will also experience conflict.

Managing Conflicts

A father and 4-year-old son are just completing a grocery store purchase when, without dad noticing, his son grabs a candy bar from the display, opens it, and begins to eat it as he follows behind his dad towards the door. Is this an episode of conflict? Why?

In this example, there are various clashes or incongruities such as between the store's policy (paying for groceries) and the child's behavior (taking groceries without paying), between a dad's desire to be perceived as an effective parent (whose children follow rules) and the child's behavior (rule-breaking), between the child's desire for immediate gratification (see candy bar, eat candy bar) and the father's desire that his son make healthy food choices (avoid sugar or consume it in moderation at appropriate times), and in larger more philosophical terms between the behaviors of a good citizen (law-abiding) and that of a criminal (law-breaking), and more. The presence of a clash or incongruity between opposing forces (in this case many clashes) make this episode one of **conflict**. And, since some of the clashes are between people (e.g. check-out clerk, father, and son) they are **interpersonal conflicts**.

Before they reach the door, the clerk yells, "Hey! Your kid took a candy bar!" and draws the situation to the father's attention. How should the dad respond? What should he say at that moment? To whom? How about later in the car? Or, when they arrive home to mom and big sister (age 10)? Or later, when an uncle stops by and comments on the situation; "What's the big deal? It was a candy bar! Boys will be boys!" What would your father say and do? What would you say and do? The setting of this episode is a public grocery store. Does it matter if the setting was at home and the child took a candy bar from the pantry?

The father's immediate response to the clerk, his son's messages, the replies from the store clerk, the father's messages to his son while in the store, in the car, and later from family members all comprise a mini-lesson for the son about how to communicate during episodes of conflict. And, whether or not the episode will serve as an example of positive communication and conflict management depends quite a lot on the message choices of the participants. Before addressing this case, let's examine children's conflicts, and then consider their negative and positive sides.

Children and Conflict Management

When do children begin fighting? What do they fight about? Lichta (2008) filmed children's play in a daycare setting and found

119

that children as young as 8-months engaged in physical struggles over the possession of objects. However, this is not the entire story as Lichta wanted to better understand their motivations for these struggles. Further analysis of her films showed children at 8, 14, and 22 months engaged in fighting but for varied motivations, the most consistent of which was the need to explore, not the need to possess. That is, young children seem to single-mindedly be driven to explore their physical world without giving much thought for others along the way! Of course exploration is a good thing, but not considering fellow explorers is something that needs attention.

How about what children learn about conflict from family interactions? E. Turner (2008) studied whether parents' conflict styles [positive problem-solving (discussion), engagement (confrontation), withdrawal, or compliance (power assertion)] at birth might later predict siblings' conflict styles at age 5. A key finding was that father's reported use of compliance or authoritarian style (at child's birth) was later associated with children's exclusive use of destructive strategies and withdrawal in sibling conflicts. Her study found clear links in parents' conflict styles as a couple and children's conflict styles with siblings. In another study, Perlman, Garfinkel, and Turrell (2007) also found that when parents used power assertion to intervene in sibling conflicts those siblings relied more heavily on destructive behaviors.

Thus, it appears that in their early years children do encounter sources of oppositional force at home and preschool, but also do not seem to pay much attention to the feelings and wellbeing of these oppositional sources. This is as it should be for toddlers who are thinking egocentrically in order to figure out their own point of view and identity. However, young children seem to gravitate toward the use of more destructive conflict styles when their parents (particularly fathers) model negative conflict management as well as use compliance (power assertion) when intervening in sibling conflicts. Conflict episodes not managed well can prompt a number of negative outcomes that include anger and aggression.

The Dark Side of Conflicts

"Anger and its expression represent a major public health problem for school-age children and adolescents" (Blake & Hamrin, 2007, p. 209). Children can express anger in the forms of violent acts, self-harm, as well as physical and verbal aggression. Anger's expression can change as children develop, with outbursts common among younger children that gradually diminish as they become capable of socialized speech and learn skills to control anger. According to Loeber (1990) uncorrected aggressive behavior in early childhood can lead to academic failure, antisocial behavior, and conduct problems in adolescence, as well as poor interpersonal relationships with peers and adults. And, aggressive behavior also increases the risk of future substance abuse. Yet, there are few intervention programs for school-age children concerning anger (most target adolescents), and research into the effectiveness of anger intervention programs is limited (Blake & Hamrin, 2007).

In terms of the family, deficits in communication and conflict resolution skills are related to a variety of negative outcomes, especially when handling conflicts with adolescents (which represents the bulk of the family conflict literature). And, although there are a few family intervention programs for use in clinical settings, they are designed to assist families in managing clinical levels of children's anger (e.g. oppositional defiant disorder, repeated violent acts, etc.), rather than teaching prosocial communication skills for use during episodes of conflict.

Finally, research suggests, "most child-abuse episodes represent direct escalations of discipline confrontations" (Reid, 1986, p. 240). That is, abusive parents resort to physically abusive behaviors after their words fail to bring about the desired result with a child, often during episodes of conflict. Wilson and his colleagues (2006) show that frequent episodes of children's repeated noncompliance followed by parents' negative physical touch is a primary pattern of abusive families that requires intervention by teaching children and parents prosocial means of managing conflicts.

The Bright Side of Conflicts

Before adults launch into managing episodes they perceive as "conflictive" with their children, it is sometimes useful to determine if the clash or incongruity is intended, or possibly the result of a communication mistake. Children (as all of us) make lots of mistakes when they are learning something new. Since eloquent, effective communication skills are difficult to acquire and practice and seem to take a lifetime to learn, mistakes are to be expected.

In the seventh grade Tom began to learn to play the trumpet in a summer band program (he later played in high-school bands, brass ensembles, and in his college's jazz band). During one summer beginning band class, his wise band director (Mr. Golden) told the band that during rehearsal he wanted them to make their mistakes good and loud. When asked why, Mr. Golden told the band this was so he could help them to correct their mistakes and improve the band's performance. He also wanted the new musicians to play fully and not hide their emerging abilities. Similar to Mr. Golden's band, film directors use many retakes of scenes before they see something they like. Unfortunately, everyday life does not seem to be like Mr. Golden's band, or film sets, in that we are not sure how to handle mistakes. To help remedy this situation and create an environment conducive to learning from mistakes as well as helping to manage potential episodes of conflict, Tom created a "**Take-2**" option in his family. That is, should someone say or do something that is perceived to be transgressive or antagonistic, Tom (or anyone in his family) can say "Take-2" which means "let's try this episode again." Take-2 gives communicators a chance to become mindful of their messages and a chance to redo them (kind of like redoing a golf shot, sometimes called taking a mulligan). After a Take-2 is requested, usually messages are quickly re-said (in more prosocial ways), but sometimes communicators will repeat the message, in which case the message is now "live" and requires management. We all make mistakes and say things that we regret. A Take-2 option can help to manage some communication episodes before they turn into conflicts.

In Chapter 4 you read about the importance of argumentation

and debate and its prosocial uses in managing power. If communicators can comfortably disagree about ideas, policies, and so on, and enter into a debate about them, while avoiding attacking the character of the debaters, then it is likely that they can come to a better understanding and make the conflict more productive. Parents and caregivers, especially those with an authoritarian style, are sometimes reluctant to hear their children disagree with them ("Hey, it's my way or the highway!"). But, asking children to help mom and dad to understand their position opens up a chance for meta-communication and reflection that can increase mindfulness for both parents and children and can create peaceful family life.

Peace is a process (Cecil & Roberts, 1995). We have to value it, practice peaceful behaviors, and learn how to restore peace when it is threatened. Cecil's book *Raising Peaceful Children in a Violent World* (1995) is an excellent resource when learning about peace as a process and the prosocial sides of conflict. Cecil's book contains exercises and activities intended to increase mindfulness about peace as well as peaceful communication practices. Among Cecil's guidelines for increasing mindfulness about peaceful communication are: "I will ask myself what part I might have played in starting or continuing an argument . . . I will say something kind to other family members as often as I can . . . I will listen to others as I would like to be listened to" (p. 47).

Summary

Have you thought about what the father might say in the grocery store situation mentioned at the start of this section? If the dad wants to be prosocial, there are a number of goals he will need to consider: First, to be collaborative, his messages must convey that he is cooperative and concerned for the images of all involved (Kilmann & Thomas, 1975). Second, he will frame the episode as a mutual problem to be managed as well as a teachable moment for his son about how to communicate during an episode of conflict. Third, his messages will support the positive identity of the participants (his son's identity, his, and the clerk's). Fourth, he will acknowledge the transgression (taking the candy bar), offer redress (returning to pay for it), and request forgiveness for the transgression on behalf of him and his son. Fifth, he will model the process of reparation for his son. Sixth, he will brighten the communication climate. Although it is *not* a good idea to diminish the seriousness of the situation by making light of it, it *is* a good idea to try to return the participants to their ease. Here is a trial message that dad might consider. Does it accomplish these goals? Does it leave anything out? You might try your hand at writing messages for dad.

> DAD [To clerk] I'm sorry. It seems that my son inappropriately began his dessert before dinner! Taking it was wrong. Let me pay for the candy bar and offer my apology on our behalf. [To son] You should not have taken that candy bar. It is wrong to take things that do not belong to us. We will talk more about why later. Here's what we have to do now: We say "sorry" to the clerk. We pay for the candy bar. Then we head to our car where we can talk more in private about this situation.

What should dad say in the car? What might the son say in response? Does what dad says depend on his son's reactions? Remember this is an opportunity to teach the son about how to manage a conflict and to fix a transgression and the messages should be thought of as a part of that lesson. Whatever messages are chosen the idea is to help the child to understand, remember, and be able to execute appropriate behaviors in the future including learning to defer gratification, showing respect for the property of others, and prosocial handling of conflict when episodes occur.

Family Communication and Development of Children's Resiliency

Resilient children learn when they need to make choices, how to generate and use resources to make optimal choices, and how to manage obstacles to optimal choice-making such as deferring gratification. Families of resilient children use the teachable moments of everyday life to help children to learn patterns of optimal decision-making, problem-solving, and prosocial conflict management. As families of resilient children make decisions, manage problems, and handle differences, they do so with an eye to the development of children's positive character traits such as those pertaining to wisdom and knowledge (e.g., creativity, perspective), courage (bravery, integrity), humanity (kindness, social intelligence), justice (fairness, social responsibility), temperance (forgiveness, self-regulation), and transcendence (gratitude, hope, and humor) (Peterson & Seligman, 2004). These kinds of positive qualities and more are forged and tested in the everyday communication habits of family life and in particular are among the many significant lessons children learn in episodes of family communication about making choices, handling problems, and managing conflicts.

In the final chapter, we offer a set of principles intended to guide families as they seek to improve their communication with children.

Activities

1. You are a parent planning a family summer vacation and want to involve a 5-year-old child in the process. Keeping in mind the developmental abilities you might expect in a 5-year-old, construct a plan for how you will involve the child in making decisions about your summer vacation. What will the plan include? What will you teach? How much say will you afford? Does the discussion differ with the gender of the child? Defend your plan by reference to the child's already mastered communication abilities as well as what they should be learning currently.

2. What strategies do you use to stay focused on important goals or projects? Try to articulate these strategies and think about how you might explain these strategies to children of various ages (say, ages 3, 5, & 7).

3. Read the following problem and answer the questions that follow.

Billy (aged 8) is invited to his new friend Tim's home to play. Tim is a new classmate of Billy who lives on his block. After checking with Tim's grandmother (who cares for the boys in afternoons), Billy's mom OK's one hour of playtime. After playing in the yard for a short while, Tim's older brother (aged 12) invites Billy and Tim into the garage where he shows them a hidden bottle of alcohol. Tim quickly takes a sip and urges Billy to try it.

What are Tim's options in this situation? What are the positive and negative sides of each option? As a parent, what messages would you suggest to Billy to handle this problem?

Suggested Further Reading

Cecil, N. L., & Roberts, P. L. (1995). *Raising peaceful children in a violent world*. San Diego, CA: LuraMedia.

Csikszentmihalyi, M., Rathunde, K., Whalen, S., & Wong, M. (1997). *Talented teenagers: The roots of success & failure*. Cambridge & New York: Cambridge University Press.

Fox, R. (2000). *Harvesting minds: How TV commercials control kids*. Westport, CT: Praeger.

Reynolds, T. J. (2005). Lifegoals: The development of a decision-making curriculum for education. *Journal of Public Policy and Marketing*, 24, 75–81. Also see: www.lifegoals.net for examples of the curriculum and lessons.

6

Children and Positive Communication Development at Home

Family communication is the first and probably the most significant context for the development of optimal communication knowledge and skills. Messages matter, especially at home, and especially those shared with children at home. In this chapter we offer our recommendations and guidance intended to help facilitate positive communication development of children as well as all family members. First, we review communication education initiatives outside the family as well as family-based interventions concerning children's communication development. Families are partners with many societal agencies (education, healthcare, recreational sports, and more) and it is important that these efforts be coordinated and mutually reinforcing (see Socha & Stamp, 2009, for studies of parent–child-societal communication). It is important that families understand what is going on concerning children's communication development outside of home (at daycare centers, schools, sports fields, and so on) and that societal agencies working with families also understand what is going on at home. Second, we outline principles intended to help guide positive communication development at home. Finally, we conclude by arguing that positive communication education is not just for children, but rather that positive communication education should stretch across the human lifespan. It is of course important to improve the foundation by focusing on improving communication in the world of children, but we also should work to improve communication of everyone – young and old.

Children's Communication Education and Family-Based Interventions

Communication Education K-12

Children learn to communicate in many contexts that include homes, playgrounds, daycare centers, friends' homes, as well as classrooms. The field of communication has devoted a great deal of research to understanding classroom communication in grades K-12, with a primary focus on helping children to meet communication competency standards at school as well as on teacher–student communication. This research is important as families and schools are partners in children's communication learning. It is important for parents to have some insights into what is going on in classrooms in terms of communication education (as well as teachers about communication at home), so that this learning might be reinforced both at home and school.

Standards of communication competency. In 1998, the National Communication Association (NCA) published *K-12 Speaking, Listening, and Media Literacy Standards and Competency Statements* (National Communication Association, 1998) that contains a list of twenty standards that cover communication-fundamentals, speaking, listening, and media literacy and is intended to assist K-12 educators in making curricular decisions. The standards are statements of general competencies such as: "Standard 4: Competent communicators demonstrate knowledge and understanding of the role of communication in creating meaning, influencing thought, and making decisions" (p. 3). Accompanying each of the twenty standards are competency statements that focus on knowledge, behaviors, and attitudes supporting the standard. A few competency statements that support Standard 4 (above) include: "distinguish between facts and opinions" (knowledge), "use language that is sensitive to individual differences" (behavior), and "appreciate how the same message may be interpreted differently by others" (attitude) (p. 7).

In general, the K-12 standards document is intended to serve as a guideline for teachers about foundational communication competencies that can be expected of children as they learn to be appropriate, effective, and ethical communicators in classrooms. "**Appropriate** [communication] . . . indicates that a communication behavior is performed within the confines of a set of expectations, guidelines, or rules, commonly agreed to by most people for the given communication situation" (p. 29). "**Effective** [communication] indicates that a communication behavior is successful in accomplishing the goals of the communicator, but may not have been performed according to appropriate guidelines" (p. 29). Thus, it is possible to communicate effectively (reach a goal), but do so inappropriately (break rules), and conversely it is possible to behave appropriately (follow the rules), but fail to reach a communication objective. "**Ethical** [communication] indicates that a communication behavior is both appropriate (respects guidelines) and effective (accomplishes goals of communicator), and that it is performed with a concern for the effect of the behavior on everyone involved" (p. 29).

For families, having an understanding of the kinds of standards and communication competencies that children will be working on as they enter school is useful insofar as families can think about how they might scaffold these competencies for children in their interactions at home. For example, how might families help young children to learn the communication standard of being able to distinguish facts from opinions? What might a mini-lesson at home about learning to tell a fact from an opinion look like? I can imagine, for instance, watching a television commercial advertising a new toy and then asking a child: Does he or she believe the message? Why? Is the message to be trusted? Why? What was really learned about the new toy? Can we trust this information? Referring back to Chapter 5, we are helping children to be better decision-makers, better consumers of media, as well as helping them to increase their communication competencies by engaging in these kinds of conversations.

Besides the communication education standards initiative for classrooms, the field of communication and related fields have developed interventions intended to help families tackle specific communication problems concerning children. Next, we discuss some of these interventions aimed at prevention of communication problems as well as enhancement of communication abilities, but first let's clarify what we mean by prevention and enhancement.

Prevention and Enhancement

Snyder and Lopez (2007) distinguish between primary and secondary prevention, where **primary prevention** "lessens or eliminates physical or psychological problems before they appear" (p. 347) and **secondary prevention** involves interventions after problems appear (to lessen and mitigate them). **Primary enhancement** refers to "establishing optimal functioning and satisfaction [and] **secondary enhancements** . . . build on already optimal functioning and satisfaction to achieve peak experiences" (p. 347). Thus, primary prevention programs concerning communication are those that seek to prevent communication problems (e.g., fear of communicating), and once problems occur, secondary preventions (e.g. psychological, medical, educational) are enlisted to stop or prevent problems from getting worse. Primary enhancement programs establish basic communication functioning of systems (e.g. how to create a positive family communication climate), while secondary enhancement programs seek to refine skills and/or target specific areas for further development (e.g., how to navigate difficult conversations such as discussions about sex, divorce, death, etc.).

Adults interested in improving their communication abilities with children can enroll in introductory college courses (e.g., children's communication, family communication), read popular literature about parenting, and attend parenting-workshops, or lectures, and more. These are examples of primary enhancement activities intended to "increase **hedonic wellbeing** by maximizing the pleasurable [communication moments with children], or to increase **eudemonic wellbeing** by setting and reaching goals [concerning helping children become better communicators]" (Snyder & Lopez, 2007, p. 361). Adult-targeted secondary enhancement communication activities can also involve enrolling in courses, workshops, lectures, and so on, but their purpose is to advance, refine, and build on already positive functions (positive communication with children, and enjoyment of the relationships).

For children, primary and secondary enhancement activities concerning communication outside the home are sometimes integrated into formal classroom instruction in language arts, health education, and social studies, but can also be found in extra-curricular activities such as school forensics and debate teams, model UN, student councils, and student ambassador programs; children's theater (at school or in the community); having children read daily announcements over the school's PA system, and the like. Children (especially those identified as somehow at risk) may also participate in short-term school-based primary interventions that target the development of an array of specific skills (e.g. saying "no" to drugs) as well as secondary enhancements that provide enrichment (e.g. school-wide multicultural awareness weeks that include talks, meals, films, and more), and so on. Outside of school, primary and secondary interventions (community-based) are also sometimes offered at community recreation centers, churches, and similar locations.

Among primary and secondary prevention and enhancement communication initiatives are a few prominent programs that seek to prevent and/or manage specific problems concerning media use, substance abuse, and negative affective disorders (depression).

Preventing the Negative Effects of Media and Enhancing the Positive

Excessive and age-inappropriate use of media (TV, computers, etc.) can harm children, and media scholars, parents, teachers, and others have been working to prevent harm and mitigate damage. Specifically, risks to children who view TV excessively can include: "increased aggressiveness . . . fear reactions . . . weight problems . . . endorsement of stereotypes" (Wilson, 2004, p. 577), and more.

Primary prevention interventions concerning children's media-use take place at home as well as at school. In general, these interventions seek to teach parents and teachers **mediation,** or ways to lessen the negative effects of exposing children to media, as well as to increase **media literacy** of children, parents, and teachers by practicing "the ability to access, analyze, evaluate, and communicate messages in a variety of forms" (Hobbs, 1997, p. 7). Meyrowitz (1998) further divided the concept of media literacy into three types: **content literacy** (critical examination of dialogue and visuals), **grammar literacy** (critical examination of production techniques, etc.), and **medium literacy** (critical examination of differences among types of media such as TV, computer, portable electronic devices). Although, full literacy includes these three dimensions, it seems that most children's media literacy efforts focus on content literacy and ignore grammar and medium literacies (possibly due to a lack of parental education concerning media literacy).

Parents, childcare providers, and teachers can choose among three kinds of mediation to increase children's media literacy: **instructive mediation** (talking with children about media harms), **restrictive mediation** (setting rules about children's media use), and **co-viewing** (parents and children viewing media together) (Wilson, 2004). Research on the relative effectiveness of these approaches suggests that instructive mediation in some form can be effective in reducing media's negative effects (Wilson, 2004). However, although co-viewing with children by itself is not as effective as instructive mediation, co-viewing is an effective tool when the subject matter prompts or is likely to prompt fear in children (Cantor, 1998, 2009).

As mentioned in earlier chapters, TV viewing is not a challenging activity – not likely to facilitate moments of flow (Csikszentmihalyi, 1990) – and contains heavy doses of adult content. Yet, children spend lots of time interacting with TV and many other forms of media:

> Young people today live media-saturated lives, spending an average of nearly 6½ hours a day (6:21) with media. Across the seven days of the week, that amount is the equivalent of a full-time job, with a few extra hours thrown in for overtime (44½ hours a week). Indeed, given that about a quarter (26%) of the time young people are using media, they're using more than one medium at a time (reading and listening to music, for example), they are actually exposed to the equivalent of 8½ hours a day (8:33) of media content, even though they pack that into less than 6½ hours of time (Kaiser, 2005).

Various professional associations warn parents about the potential risks of children's television viewing and offer guidance about ways to reduce viewing time. Among these is the American Academy of Pediatrics (AAP) that provides recommendations to pediatricians about exposing children to TV:

> Pediatricians should recommend the following guidelines for parents:
>
> 1. Limit children's total media time (with entertainment media) to no more than 1 to 2 hours of quality programming per day.
> 2. Remove television sets from children's bedrooms.
> 3. Discourage television viewing for children younger than 2 years, and encourage more interactive activities that will promote proper brain development, such as talking, playing, singing, and reading together.
> 4. Monitor the shows children and adolescents are viewing. Most programs should be informational, educational, and nonviolent.
> 5. View television programs along with children, and discuss the content. (American Academy of Pediatrics, 2001)

These guidelines echo what appears in earlier chapters: very young children learn by way of interaction, not passive observation. Furthermore, we also know that children, both young and older, benefit intellectually from the scaffolding provided by more mature viewers. The guidelines are very specific as to limiting TV exposure (two hours or less), the location of TVs in the home (TVs in children's bedrooms encourage unmonitored viewing, interfere with sleep, etc.), and the age to begin viewing (after age two). The latter guideline concerning TV viewing under age two comes from an earlier American Academy of Pediatrics policy recommendation:

> Pediatricians should urge parents to avoid television viewing for children under the age of 2 years. Although certain television programs may be promoted to this age group, research on early brain development shows that babies and toddlers have a critical need for direct interactions with parents and other significant care givers (e.g. child care providers) for healthy brain growth and the development of appropriate social, emotional, and cognitive skills. Therefore, exposing such young children to television programs should be discouraged. (American Academy of Pediatrics, 1999)

Websites Pertaining to Children's Television

- Federal Communications Commission (US) – Children's educational television policy statements such as the 1990 Children's Television Act that increased the amount of educational/instructional programming (http://www.fcc.gov/cgb/consumerfacts/childtv.html)
- National Association for the Education of Young Children (NAEYC) – Policy statement on Technology and Children (1996), available at: http://www.naeyc.org/files/naeyc/file/positions/PSTECH98.PDF
- National Institute on Media and the Family – Facts Sheet about Children and Television (http://www.mediafamily.org/facts/facts_vlent.shtml)
- PBS Parents (A website offering age-indexed viewing guides ages 3–18; translations of research studies, and more) (http://www.pbs.org/parents/childrenandmedia/)
- The Children's Media Project – an arts and education organization seeking to improve children's interactions with media (http://www.childrensmediaproject.org/index.asp)
- UNICEF – Media and Children in South Africa (information and policy statements concerning media, children, and this developing nation (http://www.unicef.org/southafrica/children_media.html)

However, the AAP is more general in their guidelines about TV content (information, educational, nonviolent) and mediation approach (co-view, instructive), and leaves decisions about what constitutes "quality programming" to parents, caregivers, and teachers.

Similar to the AAP, numerous government and nongovernmental agencies have developed recommendations for parents concerning children and media as well as offer family-based interventions (mostly primary preventions). Some of these agencies and their websites that contain useful information and recommendations appear below.

Besides TV, many others forms of electronic media are used in homes and current research is moving beyond TV to examine children's use of computers, cell phones (texting), and more. While it is early to draw solid conclusions about these media and children (see Wartella, O'Keefe, & Scantlin, 2000; Wartella, Lee, & Caplovitz, 2002), it is likely that family-based interventions will be similar to those concerning children and television use; that is, with a focus on parental mediation to prevent over-use, to prevent exposure to age-inappropriate material, to increase children's exposure to prosocial media content, as well as to increasing enlightened use.

Preventing Substance Abuse and Enhancing Health

The communication field's longest ongoing applied research project is the Drug Resistance Strategies Project (DRSP) (Hecht & Miller-Day, 2009). The DRSP is an interdisciplinary research and intervention effort lead by PENN State communication scholar Michael Hecht and his colleague, family communication scholar Michelle Miller-Day. DSRP includes numerous studies seeking to understand, develop, and test conceptual models of drug resistance, and develop and test a model for a drug resistance curriculum for middle-school children. The intervention (called *Keepin' it Real*) includes "narrative knowledge, norms, refusal skills, decision-making, risk assessment, and cultural grounding mediated by norms, attitudes, intentions, expectations, and communication competency" (Hecht & Miller-Day, 2009, p. 546). A key aspect of this research is that it incorporated ethnic culture into the model, which increased the model's effectiveness. The project is targeted for children aged 9 and above.

Among the many findings of this project, four are pertinent to our concerns about positive communication development and young children. First, direct preventative drug interventions seem best suited for students older than 5th grade (age 9–10 years). The reasons for this are primarily that most children under this age are unlikely to be offered drugs. Second, drug prevention requires work on three fronts: developing antidrug norms, decreasing positive expectancies associated with drug use, and increasing resistance skills. These fit well with our focus on positive communication development. Third, children's identity (positive and ethnic cultural) plays an important role in drug resistance (and these foundations are built early in family interaction). Hecht and Miller-Day's program's focus on ethnic culture acknowledges that approaches to talking about drugs can differ across families of varied ethnic cultural traditions and for children of varied levels of esteem. And, fourth, communication competencies play a significant role in drug offer/drug refusal episodes.

As described in Chapter 5, children will face many decisions as they grow older including whether to drink, smoke, take drugs, and so on. It is important that children be equipped with positive decision-making and communication tools to help them navigate these potentially dangerous communication episodes. Although *Keepin' it Real* is a school-based intervention, parents play a prominent role in scaffolding the foundation of skills required for successful drug resistance. For example, the *Keepin' it Real* (2009) website (http://keepinitreal.asu.edu/kir-curriculum) provides the basics of the program's four-part R.E.A.L. strategy: (1) Refuse, (2) Explain, (3) Avoid, and (4) Leave. R.E.A.L. can be useful to help children as well as parents to remember the basics when talking with middle-school children about drug resistance.

In addition to preventing the negative effects of TV viewing and substance use, prevention programs have focused on negative psychological states that include depression as well as suicidal cognitions.

Preventing Depression and Enhancing Mental Health

Psychologists who take a positive approach to child development are referred to as positive youth developmentalists. In general, taking a positive approach to mental health means helping those who are at risk for negative psychological states, such as depression, equip themselves with resources to help prevent and manage the state. One well-known positive primary prevention program designed to help children in 5th and 6th grades (aged 9–11) who are at risk for depression is grounded in Seligman's work on learned helplessness (see Gillham, Reivich, Jaycox, & Seligman, 1995). The Penn Resiliency Program (2009) was developed to help children to identify negative self-referential beliefs and to change their attributions to ones that are positive (optimistic, hopeful). More specifically,

> Through this model, students learn to detect inaccurate thoughts, to evaluate the accuracy of those thoughts, and to challenge negative beliefs by considering alternative interpretations. PRP also teaches a variety of strategies that can be used for solving problems and coping with difficult situations and emotions. Students learn techniques for assertiveness, negotiation, decision-making, social problem-solving, and relaxation. The skills taught in the program can be applied to many contexts of life, including relationships with peers and family members as well as achievement in academics or other activities. (Penn Resiliency Program, 2009)

At least thirteen controlled studies show that the PRP works at lowering incidents of depression and anxiety and that these effects can last for two more years.

Although work on the prevention of children's negative emotional states in communication has yet to emerge, it is clear from the work of positive psychologists that messages will play an important role in development of prevention programs.

Summary

There are many basic as well as advanced skills needed to both enhance the quality of everyday family life and to prevent and manage harms. In the field of communication most efforts concerning children have focused almost exclusively on the development of a few – mostly school-based – primary preventative programs, while family-based preventative programs and enhancement programs regarding children's communication skills await further development. We reviewed three examples of prevention programs concerning TV use, substance use, and depression prevention to show that family messages play a significant role in preventing and managing harms, as well as in the development of resources to support family life.

Principles of Positive Family Communication with Children

By now it should be clear that much can be learned from mindful-participation in everyday family communication. However, if family communication is to maximize its usefulness as a form of communication instruction, parents and children must become more mindful of everyday communication and its potentialities, as well as more reflective about their message choices. Here are a few principles (based on the research you have been reading) that can help increase mindfulness as well as facilitate positive communication development.

1. Families should consciously scaffold family communication episodes in order to help children to learn positive communication.

In everyday family life there are numerous "teachable moments" that potentially contain important communication lessons. By reframing everyday family communication as a form of early communication instruction, we can become more mindful of our message choices as well as their positive potential. Mindfulness helps us to pause and think before we speak, thereby making it more likely that we will choose the messages likely to have the optimal effect.

2. As parents communicate with their children, they should remember they are not only parenting, but also teaching parenting.

If we want children to become good parents one day, parenting education actually starts with parenting messages. Parents and caregivers should ask themselves: Will my message be something that I would want my child-as-a-future-parent to utter to my grandchildren? Will hearing that message in the future make me feel proud of my parenting messages? Would I use that message with children other than my own? How can I best help this child to learn about this communication episode as a communication-lesson? By educating the next generation in its earliest development, parents can truly "be the change" they wish to see in the world. Families, especially adult members, should consider children's expected levels of language, cognitive, and communicative development and adjust messages accordingly.

Children, new to communication and language skills, will be ill-prepared to compete on a level playing field with adults or older children. They will certainly try to keep up, but if they are frustrated often enough, their will to interact and learn will diminish. You know now that asking a 2-year-old to take her brother's perspective is simply setting her up for failure. Asking her to empathize with his hurt feelings is something she cannot do. Repeatedly correcting the 3-year-old's grammar will not help him learn the plural forms any faster; for him, "mouses" is the correct plural because his new rule is to add the "s" sound. So, remember that they are learning as fast as they can and they do want to interact with you in the most effective way they can muster. Simplify your sentences and modify your expectations when children are learning the ropes.

3. Families should communicate with children so as to facilitate potential and avoid communication that inhibits potential.

Along with remembering to scaffold family communication as lessons for children, it is important to be mindful of the kinds of messages these episodes contain. As you read in Chapter 2, since there are an infinite variety of ways in which messages can be constructed, it is important to examine the underlying rules that shape how they are built. Since we have framed family life (in positive terms) as agencies of potential, it follows that positive family messages are those that facilitate potentiality and negative messages as those that impede potentiality. When communicating with children, we are interacting with works-in-progress, that is, we do not know what they will be like in the future, or how the current communication episode may or may not figure into that future. But, we do know that if we adopt a positive focus and seek to add to that child's resources – or at least not diminish them – then the message value of any given episode increases. Will my message help the child's communication to develop in positive or negative ways? Will my messages help children to discover their personal strengths, or deride them and cut off exploration? Family therapist, Virginia Satir (1972; 1988) conceptualized parents as detectives whose mission was to uncover the emerging talents of their children and then to positively support the development of these talents.

4. Families should create a positive communication climate – a zone of positive proximal development – facilitative of learning, and forgiving of error.

As parents scaffold everyday family communication and use messages to facilitate children's potentialities, message mistakes are inevitable. However, if families create a communication climate where it is OK to make and learn from mistakes, then members may want to continue participating and learning. Recall that the zone of proximal development is that space between what the child can accomplish alone, and what she may accomplish with a more sophisticated interaction partner. That means that the child might be frustrated by her inability at times, but will be motivated and inspired by the model of her partner (e.g. a parent or older sibling). However, if the communication creates what has been called a **defensive climate** (Gibb, 1961), in which a blaming or insulting partner points out inadequacies, then chances are children or other members will want to go elsewhere to learn and interact.

5. Families should use communication with children as a primary force in prevention of problems, enhancement of skills, as well as increasing resilience.

From the earlier discussion of prevention and enhancement it follows that families should concentrate on developing their resources and investing in skills and experiences that will serve them in the long run. And, when skill sets are lacking, or experience needed, families must invest in primary and secondary enhancement activities to help improve and enhance skills. Here, development of future family communication enhancement programs (family-based as well as schools-based) can play a vital role for families.

6. Families should use positive communication with children as a means to increase happiness:
    a. Practice positive communication processes in everyday family life.
    b. Use communication that supports development of positive character traits.
    c. Use positive communication coaching to assist children as they grapple with problematic communication outside and within the home.

Positive communication processes include: empathic listening, prosocial humor (nice jokes), communicative support, forgiveness, compliments, prayer, and more (Socha & Pitts, in review). And, as Gottman and colleagues have shown (Gottman, Declaire, & Goleman, 1998), parents can serve as emotion coaches for their children by teaching them about the kinds of emotions humans experience and helping them to encourage positive emotional states and manage negative ones.

Communication with children can also support development of positive character strengths (Peterson & Seligman, 2004). This represents an important frontier in positive family communication. Peterson and Seligman (2004), in their monumental book: *Character strengths and virtues: A handbook and classification* developed a system that organized positive character into six core moral virtues (wisdom/knowledge, courage, humanity, justice, temperance, and transcendence) and 24 character strengths under each virtue. For example, the character strengths that underscore courage include: bravery, persistence, integrity (honesty), and vitality (zest, enthusiasm). Further, Peterson and Seligman (using Erickson's classic stages of development) offered a preliminary developmental map that included a consideration of character strengths by age: Birth–age 1: hope, gratitude; Ages 1–3: persistence; Ages 3–6: curiosity; and Ages 6–puberty: love of learning, creativity. Our basic recommendations for parents to communicate positively, openly and authoritatively go a long way toward supporting these character strengths.

A Lifetime of Communication Development

Although this book has focused on the foundation of communication development by examining young children, communication development is in reality a lifespan phenomenon – from our very first messages to our last. Across the lifespan it is always possible to further hone our communicating skills and engage in communication processes more effectively. When psychologists first started studying children's development, they assumed that development was pretty complete at the end of the teen years. However, people change physically, cognitively, and communicatively throughout life. Many of the really significant changes in the way we view the world and act in it are the result of dialogues we have with others – intimate others, especially family. One suggestion for an ethic of communication development is: "Be responsible for self, nurture others, and contribute to the future" (Yingling, 2004, p. 332). In parenting, we find an opportunity to be responsible for our own continuing development, to nurture those who most need it, and to contribute to the future in a very personal way. Nothing is more ethical when done well than parenting.

Given the ongoing nature of communication development, it is of course important to make sure that our first communication steps are on a solid footing. In this spirit, we offer five reasons to place children and their communication nurturance at the top of our priority list for families and societal agencies that support families. First, early communication intervention helps prevent later communication problems. Second, early communication education increases the chances of developing sound communication fundamentals for use in the future. Third, early communication education builds a platform for the development of advanced communication understandings and skills. Fourth, early communication education can teach positive communication values as part of the foundation of communication education. And fifth, focusing on positive communication development early in a child's life can increase the chances that he or she will attain positive individual goals such as: creating and maintaining a positive identity, understanding and adhering to prosocial norms, recognizing positive behavior, and more (see Catalono, Berglund, Ryan, Lonczak, & Hawkins, 1998).

Since communication learning continues beyond childhood we encourage families at all points of the family life cycle to be mindful of their communication. We also urge the communication field to continue to develop ways to support families as they develop their communication abilities. Such support could include a greater presence of children in college communication curricula (in texts and courses), a greater emphasis on communication development in high schools (public speaking as well as interpersonal, group communication, and media use skills), as well as a continued focus on cultivating effective communication skills of elementary and pre-K students. We encourage parents and future parents to keep educating themselves about children's communication, and to keep practicing positive communication to make it a habit. We trust that in the future, our cultural mores and political system will increasingly support positive family communication, and continue to see that children are family communicators too.

Activities

1. Select one positive communication process discussed in the book, such as empathic listening and write a family communication education curriculum for its development. What does empathic listening development look like? What might families do to encourage its members to value empathic listening?

What kinds of family activities might facilitate the development of empathic listening abilities?

2. Develop plans for positive media use employing instructional, restrictive, and co-viewing mediation for families with children in the following age groups: ages 0–3, 4–6, and 7–10.

3. Develop your own list of positive family communication competencies. Which ones should be included? Which ones are more important to emphasize? Why?

4. Reflect on the principles of children's positive communication development in light of your family's communication. To what extent did your family emphasize the principles? Can you recall examples of when they communicated in ways that were consistent with the principles? How might these episodes have shaped your communication?

5. Reflect on the principles of children's positive communication development in family communication portrayed in television shows. For example, you might view episodes of TV families from different historical periods and compare them (e.g. *Leave it to Beaver* and *The Simpsons*).

Suggested Further Reading

Gottman, J., Declaire, J., & Goleman, D. (1998). *Raising an emotionally intelligent child*. New York: Simon & Schuster.

National Communication Association (1998). *K-12 speaking, listening, and media literacy standards and competency statements*. Washington, DC: National Communication Association. Available at http://www.natcom.org/nca/files/ccLibraryFiles/FILENAME/000000000119/K12%20Standards.pdf.

Satir, V. (1988). *The new peoplemaking*. Mountain View, CA: Science and Behavior Books.

Socha, T. J., & Stamp, G. H. (eds) (2009). *Parents and children communicating with society: Managing relationships outside of home*. New York: Routledge.

Van Evra, J. (2004). *Television and child development*. Mahwah, NJ: Lawrence Erlbaum.

Glossary

Note: Unless otherwise noted, definitions were coined by the authors, or adopted from Yingling, 2004.

Accommodation: occurs by changing the internal system to adapt to information that doesn't quite fit into the present system.

ACL: Adult–child language or speech adapted to the child's needs. Usually consists of exaggerated intonation, higher pitch, and slowed tempo.

Affect: A general term referencing feelings from simple arousal to symbolic emotion.

Appropriate communication: "indicates that a communication behavior is performed within the confines of a set of expectations, guidelines, or rules, commonly agreed to by most people for the given communication situation" (NCA, 1998, p. 29).

Argumentativeness: A willingness to present and defend one's position; implies a willingness to listen to another's position as well.

Assimilation: involves taking and using information from an external environment.

Attachment: The bond created in interaction between the child and the primary caregiver(s). According to attachment theorists, the nature of this bond influences later relationships and psychological adjustment.

Authoritarian: A parenting style characterized by assertion of power: demanding, directive, unresponsive to child's desires or arguments.

Glossary

Authoritative: Parenting style characterized by communicating facts and insights, a willingness to receive a child's reasoned argument. These parents use reason and encourage verbal give and take.

Behaviorists: Scholars who adhere to the tenet, humans learn by soaking up stimuli from their surroundings via some form of conditioning.

Bias: Unwanted and/or unintended influences on a decisional choice.

Bi-residential: a situation referring to children living in multiple households at the same time.

Blended family: a term for a kind of stepfamily that carries fewer negative connotations, and emphasizes the integration of new members to the family.

Boomerang child: An adult who returns to the childhood home.

Categorization: The ability to group qualities into one cluster. For example, using the word "table" for any item with four legs supporting a horizontal, flat surface.

Childhood: A prolonged period of development characterized by relative protection from the adult world.

Choice: expression of preference, that is, when I choose one kind of soft drink rather than another, at that moment I am telling the world that I prefer or value this particular soft drink.

Cognition: A general term for mental operations, including the use of concepts in thought and analysis by categorization and differentiation.

Cognitive complexity: The number and organizational complexity of constructs available to an individual.

Cohesiveness (families): refers to the psychological closeness members of a family (group) feel towards each other.

Communication: Acknowledging input to perception. "That which links any organism together" (Cherry, 1966, p. 36) whether that organism is a pair of friends, a mother and child, or an "American Idol" star and her audience.

Complex family: A family system characterized by high integration (interdependence) and high differentiation (autonomy); whereas a **simple family** experiences low levels of both integration (higher control; weaker sense of self) and differentiation (higher dependence) (adapted from Rathunde & Csikszentmihalyi, 1991, p. 144).

Glossary

Conflict: clash or incongruity concerning communication-styles, opinions, facts, policies, and/or scarce resources.

Conjoint decisions: choices shared by two or more individuals.

Construct: A reference axis made up of two poles of meaning; the basis of differentiation used to establish a personal orientation toward people (or things).

Consummate love: In Sternberg's (1986) theory of love the result of combining all three dimensions (intimacy, passion, commitment).

Content literacy: a form of media literacy that focuses on dialogue and visuals (Meyrowitz, 1998).

Control: The employment of regulatory capacities, including regulation of self, of others and of the environment.

Co-regulation occurs "whenever individuals' joint actions blend together to achieve a unique and mutually created set of social actions" (Fogel, 1993, p. 6).

Co-viewing: a form of mediation that centers on parents and children sharing media viewing experiences (Wilson et al., 2006).

Created family: A collective of people who voluntarily choose commitment to the support and development of family members (adapted from Weston, 1991).

Creativity: "an act, idea, or product that changes an existing domain or that transforms an existing domain into a new one" (Csikszentmihalyi, 1996, p. 28).

Critical period: "A period of development during which certain events must take place if they are to take place at all" (Gleason, 1993, p. 455).

Decentration: "the ability to see or to see activities and relationships from other than a purely selfish point of view" (Dance & Larson, 1976, p. 68). To **decenter** is to see from another's point of view.

Decision-making: selecting a choice from among alternatives.

Defensive climate: created when a blaming or insulting partner points out inadequacies (adapted from Gibb, 1961).

Deixis: Communication by pointing out things in the environment, literally by gesture, or in deictic words (e.g. "here," "there.")

Development: the process of change in secondary (symbolic) systems, including emotional, cognitive and communicative complexes, which rely on the maturation of primary (biological) systems as well as interaction with other symbol-users.

Dialectics: The tension between two opposing but related positions. In terms of symbols, this explains the notion of a construct such as "happy/sad" whereby either pole would have no meaning without the other.

Differentiation: The developmental process by which an individual comes to perceive each object as separate and distinct from others. Linked to the contrast inherent in symbolic meaning.

Effective communication: "indicates that a communication behavior is successful in accomplishing the goals of the communicator, but it may not have been performed according to appropriate guidelines" (NCA, 1998, p. 29).

Egocentric speech: Speech produced for one's own purposes alone; not adapted for the listener.

Egocentrism: The views from one's own sensory system; or the inability to view activities or relationships from other than one's own point of view.

Elaborated codes: semantically abstract and syntactically complex language usage.

Emotions: Specific mental states referencing some affective experience, usually with symbols.

Empathy: The capacity to feel what another is feeling, at the same time recognizing that the other's feeling is separate from one's own.

Ethical communication: "indicates that a communication behavior is both appropriate (respects guidelines) and effective (accomplishes goals of communicator), and that it is performed with a concern for the effect of the behavior on everyone involved" (NCA, 1998, p. 29).

Eudemonic wellbeing: functioning and happiness related to setting and reaching goals.

Expected values: In decision-making theory, the relative value that is anticipated from an alternative in a decisional choice.

Family: a nexus of individuals linked by consent or birth who collaborate in the creation and continuation of family identity and in the development of the potentialities of the system, its relationships, and its members (adapted from Socha, 2006).

Family authority: Legitimate power or an agreement that gives adults the rights and responsibilities of leading family systems.

Family climate: refers to family members' "perceptions of the relative warmth or coldness that characterizes the interpersonal relationships among members (Scheerhorn & Geist, 1997, p. 91).

Family governance: Structures of interaction where leaders and followers set goals, endorse values, make policies, develop procedures, and direct the behaviors of members.

Gender role: Sets of expected behaviors organized according to masculinity-femininity.

Gender role socialization: the process of learning gender roles.

Grammar literacy: a form of media literacy that focuses on production techniques and language of a medium (Meyrowitz, 1998).

Group social processes: pertain to family-group relationships such as cohesiveness (closeness-distance) and climate (warmth-coldness).

Group task processes: processes that pertain to goal-directed activities such as making decisions, solving problems, and leadership.

Hedonic treadmill: the process of adapting to a state of pleasure and requiring increased stimulation to return to future pleasurable states.

Hedonic wellbeing: functioning and happiness related to maximizing what is pleasurable.

Heuristic: a rule of thumb or shortcut used in processing information relevant to a decisional choice.

Identity: A developmental process of constituting meaning for self, based on repeated internalizations of external interaction, and the communicative performances subsequent to those interactions that express, reaffirm, or reject the self-meanings so constituted.

Indicating: Communication designed to bring the partner's attention to something.

Individuation: The developmental process whereby one gradually perceives self as more and more clearly separate from others.

Inner speech: speech for self that is covert, silent, and purposeful.

Instructive mediation: a form of mediation that centers on talking with children about media harms (Meyrowitz, 1998).

Internalization: The process of bringing external experience into one's core (mind) where it may be stored in symbols and restructured.

Interactionists: Scholars who embrace the notion that both nature and nurture contribute to human development. In particular, this school of thought holds that human interaction per se is necessary to human development, cognitive, social, and communicative.

Interpersonal conflict: clash or incongruity concerning communication styles, opinions, facts, policies, and/or scarce resources that takes place between two or more people.

Intuitive parenting: Natural parental responses to stable inborn characteristics of very young infants. These range from strong body stimulation to soothe a crying infant, to vocalizations and eye contact in response to infant cooing.

Maturation: The biological process of development; the growth of physical structures.

Media literacy: "the ability to access, analyze, evaluate, and communicate messages in a variety of forms" (Hobbs, 1997, p. 7).

Mediation: ways to lessen the negative effects of exposing children to media.

Medium literacy: a form of media literacy that focuses on differences among types of media (such as TV, computer, portable electronic devices).

Myelinate: to form a protective sheath that accumulates along nerve fibers enhancing the rapid transmission of neural impulses.

Nativists: A descriptive term for those scholars who adhere to the tenet that much of human behavior may be explained by human physiology, including brain and nervous system as well as sound-making capacities and fine motor abilities.

Negation: The ability to refer to a state of nonexistence; to contrast what *is* with what is *not*. In its most primitive form at around two years, the simple "No" in response to just about anything.

Nuclear family: The current normative standard family; a married couple, man and woman, and their biological offspring.

Nurture: The process of providing care for another.

Open system: systems with boundaries that are permeable or open to the outside world.

Other-awareness: The process whereby one perceives another as independent from self, and eventually, as distinct from all others.

Parentification: Process of children over-playing the role of parent.

Permissive: A parenting style characterized by responsiveness with few demands. These are the least likely parents to offer facts and most likely to use guilt to control or to simply give in to a pleading child (also known as "laissez-faire" parenting).

Perspective-taking: The cognitive capacity to adopt another's point of view.

Phonetics: The study of the smallest distinctive speech sounds that humans use to signal meaning.

Pleasure: "encompasses a family of subjective positive psychological states that range from 'raw feels of the body' . . . to higher pleasures of the mind occasioned by Beethoven's Ninth symphony . . ." (Peterson, 2006, p. 48).

Polygamy: A family configuration composed of multiple adults and their biological offspring. Possible variations include **Polygyny** – one husband, several wives, **polyandry** – one wife, several husbands, and **polygynandry** – group marriage.

Positive approach to family communication: examines the communication processes that create the optimal conditions for the development of human capacities across the lifespan.

Power: "the ability to act or affect [someone or something]" (*Oxford English Dictionary*, 2009).

Power base: A resource that can be used in power interactions, like authority, rewards, and punishments.

Power outcomes: What results from power interactions including decisions, solutions, new rules or procedures, as well as emotional outcomes like how participants feel about decisions, solutions, or rules, as well as themselves and each other.

Power processes: Refers to how power is used in interactions.

Pragmatics: The study of how things (e.g. rituals, relationships, self-presentation) are accomplished with language and communication.

Predication: Asserting something about a thing of interest; the comment about a topic.

Primary enhancement refers to "establishing optimal functioning and satisfaction" (Snyder & Lopez, 2007, p. 347).

Primary prevention: "lessens or eliminates physical or psychological problems before they appear" (Snyder & Lopez, 2007, p. 347).

Private speech: Speech used to solve problems aloud that have not yet been internalized characterized by abbreviation and predication.

Problems: situations where alternatives are either unknown or not yet clearly understood. Can be **life-threatening, major, minor**, as well as **acute** or **chronic.**

Problem-solving: process of identifying (often inventing) alternatives so that decision-making can proceed.

Protosymbols: early meaning constructions based on categorizing, differentiating, and generalizing meaning. Typically using joint referencing to call attention to a thing; not yet using predication to comment on a thing or event.

Relational dialectics: are the tensions we experience in the push/pull of relationships, such as: autonomy/integration, novelty/predictability, openness/closedness. Family dialectics are similar, but include a love/hostility dialectic, inevitable in intimate, nonvoluntary relationship sets.

Relationship: A connection between two distinct selves, constructed by both symbolic and nonsymbolic interaction, and constituted dialogically.

Representation: The ability to use one thing to stand for another. For example, humans often use sounds to represent things, ideas, events. But we can as easily use objects including written codes to do the same.

Resiliency: "patterns of positive adaptation in the context of significant adversity or risk" (Masten & Reed, 2002, p. 75).

Restrictive codes: semantically condensed and syntactically simple language usage.

Restrictive mediation: a form of mediation that involves setting rules about children's media use (Wilson, 2004).

Role: A set of expected behaviors, or a framework of instructions that guide individuals playing a particular part.

Role play: Practicing a set of behaviors one has associated with an observed social role.

Rule: followable prescription for what behaviors are obligated, preferred, prohibited in social situations (Shimanoff, 1980).

Scaffold(ing): The process of structuring interaction to maximize a child's learning.

Script: A scaffold for social behavior; a set of standard routines for social activity.

Secondary enhancements: "build on already optimal functioning and satisfaction to achieve peak experiences" (Snyder & Lopez, 2007, p. 347).

Secondary prevention: "lessens or eliminates physical or psychological problems after they appear" (Snyder & Lopez, 2007, p. 347).

Semantics: The study of the meanings attached to sets of phonemes (sounds).

Signature strengths: In positive psychology refers to individuals' talents and abilities that are an important part of an individual's identity.

Skills: Behavior sets developed for their usefulness in reaching goals. These may be acquired through trial and error or training.

Sociality: The function of communicating performances among identities; sharing one's idea of self and receiving another's idea of self.

Socialization: The process of learning to imagine another's point of view. The flip side of egocentrism.

Socially constructed: refers to the symbolic and interactive processes of building meaning and understanding relationships.

Socialized speech: Speech produced in recognition of, and adapted to, the interacting other.

Spoken language: "The fusion of genetically determined speech with culturally determined language." Language, then, is the "syntactic systematization of signs and/or symbols" (Dance, 1982, p. 126).

Stepfamily: A family configuration in which at least two adults care for at least one child who is not the biological offspring of both adults (adapted from Turner & West, 2002).

Strategies: Ways of thinking about problems encountered in the pursuit of goals that assist in overcoming those problems. Strategies can become habitual, but can also be highly creative.

Subjective probability: In decision-making theory this refers to the chances that the rewards or costs of an alternative will materialize.

Symbol: "A stimulus whose relationship with that with which it is associated is a result of the decision or arbitrary agreement of human user(s)" (Dance, 1982, p. 126).

Syntax: The structural properties of language; the rules that allow us to recognize parts of speech and their order to express complete ideas.

Take-2: a communication "redo," should someone say or do something that is perceived to be transgressive or antagonistic.

Turn-taking: The prerequisite for conversation; the willingness and skill to both listen and wait for an appropriate time to speak, and to assume the conversational floor.

Verbal aggression: Attacking the self-concept of another (Infante & Wigley, 1986). May take the form of insults, teasing, threats; amounts to verbal abuse.

Zone of proximal development: "the range of behaviors available to a child in the helpful presence of a guiding adult" (Gleason, 1993, p. 467).

References

Adler, A. (1956). *The individual psychology of Alfred Adler: A systematic presentation in selections from his writings.* Edited and annotated by H. L. Ansbacher & R. R. Ansbacher. New York: Basic Books.

Allen, M., & Burrell, N. (1996). Comparing the impact of homosexual and heterosexual parents on children: Meta-analysis of existing research. *Journal of Homosexuality, 32*(2), 19–33.

American Academy of Pediatrics (1999). Policy statement: American Academy of Pediatrics Committee on Public Education – Children adolescents and television. *Pediatrics, 104* (2), 341–343. Abstract available at http://aappolicy.aappublications.org/cgi/content/full/pediatrics;104/2/341.

American Academy of Pediatrics (2001). Policy statement: American Academy of Pediatrics Committee on Public Education – Children adolescents and television. *Pediatrics, 107* (2), 423–426. Abstract available at http://aappolicy.aappublications.org/cgi/content/full/pediatrics;107/2/423.

Antonucci, T. C. (2001). Social relations: An examination of social networks, social support and sense of control. In J. E. Birren & K. W. Shaie (eds), *Handbook of the psychology of aging* (5th edn, pp. 427–453). New York: Academic Press.

Applegate, J. L., Burleson, B. R., & Delia, J. G. (1992). Reflection-enhancing parenting as antecedent to children's social-cognitive and communicative development. In I. E. Sigel, A.V. McGillicuddy-Delisi, & J. J. Goodnow (eds). *Parental belief systems: The psychological consequences for children* (2nd edn, pp. 3–39). Hillsdale, NJ: Lawrence Erlbaum.

Aslin, R. N. (1987). Visual and auditory development in infancy. In J. D. Osofsky (ed.), *Handbook of infant development* (2nd edn, pp. 5–97). New York: Wiley.

Bandura, A. (1977). *Social learning theory.* Englewood Cliffs, NJ: Prentice Hall.

Barton, M., & Tomasello, M. (1991). Joint attention and conversation in mother–infant–sibling triads. *Child Development, 62*, 517–529.

155

References

Basile, R. (1974). Lesbian mothers I. *Women's Rights Law Reporter, 2*, 3–18.

Baskett, L. M. (1984). Ordinal position differences in children's family interactions. *Developmental Psychology, 20*, 1026–1031.

Baumrind, D. (1968). Authoritarian vs. authoritative parental control. *Adolescence, 3*, 255–272.

Baumrind, D. (1971). Current patterns of parental authority. *Developmental Psychology Monographs, 4*(1).

Baxter, L. A., Braithwaite, D. O., Bryant, L. E., & Wagner, A. (2004). Stepchildren's perceptions of the contradictions in communication with stepparents. *Journal of Social and Personal Relationships, 21*, 447–467.

Baxter, L. A., & Montgomery, B. M. (1996). *Relating: Dialogues and dialectics*. New York: Guilford.

Baxter, L. A., Braithwaite, D. O., & Nicholson, J. H. (1999). Turning points in the development of blended families. *Journal of Social and Personal Relationships, 16*(3), 291–313.

Bayer, C. L., & Cegala, D. J. (1992). Trait verbal aggressiveness and argumentativeness: Relations with parenting style. *Western Journal of Communication, 56*, 301–310.

Beatty, M. J., & McCroskey, J. C. (2000). A few comments about communibiology and the nature/nurture question. *Communication Education, 49*, 25–28.

Beck, U., & Beck-Gernsheim, E. (2002). *Individualization*. London: Sage.

Belsky, J., Fish, M., & Isabella, R. (1991). Continuity and discontinuity in infant negative and positive emotionality: Family antecedents and attachment consequences. *Developmental Psychology, 27* (3), 421–431.

Belsky, J., Ward, M. J., & Rovine, M. (1986). Prenatal expectations, postnatal experiences and the transition to parenthood. In R. Ashmore & D. Brodinsky (eds), *Thinking about the family: Views of parents and children* (pp. 119–145). Hillsdale, NJ: Lawrence Erlbaum.

Berk, L. E. (1998). *Development through the lifespan*. Needham Heights, MA: Allyn & Bacon.

Bernstein, B. (1971). *Class, codes and control* (Vol. 1). London: Routledge & Kegan Paul.

Bernstein, B. (1973). *Class, codes and control* (Vol. 2). London: Routledge & Kegan Paul.

Bernstein, B. (1977). *Class, codes and control* (Vol. 3, 2nd edn). London: Routledge & Kegan Paul.

Birkerts, S. (1994). *The Gutenberg elegies*. NY: Fawcett Columbine.

Blake, C. S., & Hamrin, V. (2007). Current approaches to the assessment and management of anger and aggression in youth: A review. *Journal of Child and Adolescent Psychiatric Nursing, 20*, 209–221.

Bloom, K., & Lo, E. (1990). Adult perceptions of vocalizing infants. *Infant Behavior and Development, 13*, 209–219.

Bornstein, M. H., Tal, J., & Rahn, C. (1992). Functional analysis of the contents of

References

maternal speech to infants of 5 to 13 months in four cultures: Argentina, France, Japan, and the United States. *Developmental Psychology, 28*(4), 593–603.

Bozett, F. (1987). Children of gay fathers. In F. Bozett (ed.), *Gay and lesbian parents* (pp. 38–57). New York: Praeger.

Braithwaite, D. O., McBride, M. C., & Schrodt, P. (2003). "Parent teams" and the everyday interactions of co-parenting in stepfamilies. *Communication Reports, 16*, 93–111.

Braithwaite, D. O., Schrodt, P., & Baxter, L. A. (2006). Understudied and misunderstood: Communication in stepfamily relationships. In K. Floyd & M. T. Morman (eds). *Widening the family circle: New Research on family communication.* Thousand Oaks, CA: Sage.

Brand, R. J., Shallcross, W. L., Sabatos, M. G., & Massie, K. P. (2007). Fine-grained analysis of motionese: Eye gaze, object exchanges, and action units in infant-versus adult-directed action. *Infancy, 11* (2), 203–214.

Bray, J. H., & Kelly, J. (1998). *Stepfamilies: Love, marriage, and parenting in the first decade.* New York: Broadway.

Brazelton, T. B. (1973). *Neonatal behavioral assessment scale.* Philadelphia: Lippencott.

Brody, G. H., Stoneman, Z., & Burke, M. (1987). Child temperaments, maternal differential behavior, and sibling relationships. *Developmental Psychology, 23*, 354–362.

Bruner, J. (1975). From communication to language – A psychological perspective. *Cognition, 3*, 255–287.

Bruner, J. (1977). Early social interaction and language acquisition. In H. R. Schaffer (eds), *Culture, communication and cognition: Vygotskian perspectives* (pp. 21–34). Cambridge, UK: Cambridge University Press.

Bruner, J. (1983). *Child's talk: Learning to use language.* New York: Norton.

Burleson, B. R. (1994). Comforting messages: Significance, approaches, and effects. In B. R. Burleson, T. L. Albrecht, & I. G. Sarason (eds) *Communication of social support* (pp. 3–28). Thousand Oaks, CA: Sage.

Burleson, B. R., & Kunkel, A. (1996). The socialization of emotional support skills in childhood. In G. R. Pierce, B. S. Sarason, & I. G. Sarason (eds), *Handbook of social support and the family* (pp. 105–140). New York: Plenum Press.

Burton, L. M. (1992). Black grandparents rearing children of drug-addicted parents: Stressors, outcomes, and social service needs. *The Gerontologist, 32*(6), 744–751.

Byng-Hall, J. (2002). Relieving parentified children's burdens in families with insecure attachment patterns. *Family Process, 41,* 375–388.

Byng-Hall, J. (2008). The significance of children fulfilling parental roles: Implications for family therapy. *Journal of Family Therapy, 30,* 147–162.

Camras, L. A., Malatesta, C., & Izard, C. (1991). The development of facial expression in infancy. In R. Feldman & B. Rime (eds), *Fundamentals of nonverbal behavior.* New York: Cambridge University Press.

References

Canary, D. J., & Hause, K. (1993). Is there any reason to research sex differences in communication? *Communication Quarterly, 41,* 129–144.

Canary, D. J., Cupach, W. R., & Messman, S. J. (1995). *Relationship conflict.* Thousand Oaks, CA: Sage.

Cantor, J. (1998). *"Mommy I'm scared": How TV and movies frighten children and what we can do to protect them.* New York: Harcourt Brace.

Cantor, J. (2009). *Your mind on media: Information for families.* Available at http://yourmindonmedia.com/families.php.

Cassell, J., & Ryokai, K. (2001). Making space for voice: Technologies to support children's fantasy and storytelling. *Personal Technologies, 5,* 203–224.

Catalono, R. F., Berglund, M. L., Ryan, J. A. M., Lonczak, H. S. & Hawkins, J. D. (1998). *Positive youth development in the United States: Research findings on evaluations of youth development programs.* Retrieved July 21, 2009 from http://aspe.hhs.gov/hsp/PositiveYouthDev99/.

Cecil, N. L., & Roberts, P. L. (1995). *Raising peaceful children in a violent world.* San Diego, CA: LuraMedia.

Cernoch, J. M., & Porter, R. H. (1985). Recognition of maternal axillary odors by infants. *Child Development, 56,* 1593–1598.

Chaney, C. (1994). Language development, metalinguistic awareness, and emergent literacy skills of 3-year-old children in relation to social class. *Applied Psycholinguistics 15*(3), 371–394.

Cherlin, A., & Furstenberg, F. F. (1986). Grandparents and family crisis. *Generations, 10,* 26–28.

Cherry, C. (1966). The communication of information. In A. G. Smith (ed.), *Communication and culture.* New York: Holt, Rinehart and Winston.

Chomsky, N. (1965). *Aspects of the theory of syntax.* Cambridge, MA: MIT Press.

Chiu, S., & Alexander, P. A. (2000). The motivational function of preschoolers' private speech. *Discourse Processes, 30* (2), 133–152.

Cissna, K. M., Cox, D. E., & Bochner, A. P. (1990). The dialectic of marital and parental relationships within the stepfamily. *Communication Monographs, 57,* 44–61.

Clay, J. W. (1990). Respecting and supporting gay and lesbian parents. *Young Children, 45,* 31–35.

Coleman, M., Ganong, L., & Fine, M. (2004). Communication in stepfamilies. In A. Vangelisti (ed.), *Handbook of family communication* (215–232). Mahwah, NJ: Lawrence Erlbaum.

Coley, R. L. (2001). (In)visible men: Emerging research on low-income, unmarried, and minority fathers. *American Psychologist, 56*(9), 743–753.

Combs-Orme, T, & Renkert, L. E. (2009). Fathers and their infants: Caregiving and affection in the modern family. *Journal of Human Behavior in the Social Environment, 19* (4), 394–418.

Condon, J. T., & Corkindale, C. J. (2008). Assessment of postnatal paternal-infant attachment: Development of a questionnaire instrument. *Journal of Reproductive and Infant Psychology, 26* (3), 195–210.

Cook-Gumperz, J. (1973). *Social control and socialization.* London: Routledge & Kegan Paul.

Csikszentmihalyi, M. (1990). *Flow: The psychology of optimal experience.* New York: HarperCollins.

Csikszentmihalyi, M. (1996). *Creativity: Flow and the psychology of discovery and invention.* New York: HarperPerennial.

Csikszentmihalyi, M., Rathunde, K., Whalen, S., & Wong, M. (1997). *Talented teenagers: The roots of success & failure.* Cambridge & New York: Cambridge University Press.

Curtiss, S. (1977). *Genie: A psycholinguistic study of a modern-day "wild child."* New York: Academic Press.

Daly, J. A., Vangelisti, A. L., & Daughton, S. M. (1987). The nature and correlates of conversational sensitivity. *Human Communication Research, 14*(2), 167–202.

Dance, F. E. X. (1982). A speech theory of human communication. In F. E. X. Dance (ed.), *Human communication theory.* New York: Harper & Row.

Dance, F. E. X., & Larson, C. E. (1976). *The functions of human communication: A theoretical approach.* New York: Holt, Rinehart and Winston.

DeCasper, A. & Spence, M. (1986). Prenatal maternal speech influences newborns' perception of speech sounds. *Infant Behavior and Development 9,* 113–150.

Delia, J. G., & Clark, R. A. (1977). Cognitive complexity, social perception, and the development if listener-adapted communication in six-, eight-, ten-, and twelve-year-old boys. *Communicating Monographs, 44,* 326–345.

Delia, J. G., Kline, S., & Burleson, B. (1979). The development of persuasive communication strategies in kindergartners through twelfth graders. *Communication Monographs, 46,* 241–256.

Dill, K. E., & Dill, J. C. (1998). Video game violence: A review of the empirical literature. *Aggression and Violent Behavior 3,* 407–428.

Dindia, K. (1998). "Going into and coming out of the closet": The dialectics of stigma disclosure. In B. M. Montgomery & L. A. Baxter (eds), *Dialectical approaches to studying personal relationships* (pp. 83–108). Mahwah, NJ: Lawrence Erlbaum.

Dixson, M. D. (1995). Models and perspectives of parent–child communication. In T. J. Socha & G. H. Stamp (eds), *Parents, children and communication: Frontiers of theory and research* (pp. 43–62). Hillsdale, NJ: Lawrence Erlbaum.

Dixson, M. D., & Stein, A. (1997, June). *Children's models of the parent–child relationships: What do young children expect?* Paper presented at the International Network of Personal Relationships, Oxford, Ohio.

Dore, J. (1974). A pragmatic description of early language development. *Journal of Psycholinguistics Research, 3,* 343–350.

References

Dunn, J. (1988). Connections between relationships: Implications of research on mothers and

Dunn, J. (1991). The developmental importance of differences in siblings' experiences within the family. In K. Pillemer & K. McCartney (eds), *Parent–child relations throughout life* (pp. 113–124). Mahwah, NJ: Lawrence Erlbaum.

Dunn, J. (1993). *Young children's close relationships: Beyond attachment.* Newbury Park, CA: Sage.

Dunn, J., & Kendrick, C. (1982). *Siblings: Love, envy, and understanding.* Cambridge, MA: Harvard University Press.

Dunn, J., & Munn, P. (1985). Becoming a family member: Family conflict and the development of social understanding in the second year. *Child Development, 56,* 480–492.

Dunn, J., & Munn, P. (1986). Siblings and prosocial development. *International Journal of Behavioral Development, 9,* 265–284.

Dunn, J., & Munn, P. (1987). The development of justification in disputes with another sibling. *Developmental Psychology, 23,* 791–798. *Early Years: An International Journal of Research and Development, 28,* 235–249.

Eimas, P. D., Siqueland, E. R., Jusczyk, P., & Vigorito, J. (1971). Speech perception in infants. *Science, 171,* 303–306.

Elkind, D. (1974). *A sympathetic understanding of the child: Birth to sixteen.* Boston: Allyn & Bacon.

Emery, R. E., & Dillon, P. (1994). Conceptualizing the divorce process: Renegotiating boundaries of intimacy and power in the divorce family system. *Family Relations, 43,* 374–379.

Epstein, N. B., Bishop, D. S., & Baldwin, L. M. (1982). McMaster model of family functioning. In F. Walsh (ed.), *Normal family processes* (pp. 115–141). New York: Guilford.

Financial Services Authority (2009). Calculator 2 cost of a child. Retrieved June 15, 2009 from http://www.fsa.gov.uk/financial_capability/pgtm/parents/fmf/calculators/calculator2.html.

Finger, B., Hans, S. L., Bernstein, V. J., & Cox, S. M. (2009). Parent relationship quality and infant–mother attachment. *Attachment and Human Development, 11* (3), 285–306.

Floyd, K., & Morman, M. T. (2006). *Widening the family circle: New research on family communication.* Thousand Oaks, CA: Sage.

Fogel, A. (1993). *Developing through relationships: Origins of communication, self, and culture.* Chicago: University of Chicago Press.

Forman, E. A., & Cazden, C. B. (1985). Exploring Vygotskian perspectives in education: The cognitive value of peer interaction. In J. V. Wertsch (ed.), *Culture, communication and cognition: Vygotskian perspectives* (pp. 323–347). Cambridge, UK: Cambridge University Press.

Fox, R. (2000). *Harvesting minds: How TV commercials control kids.* Westport, CT: Praeger.

References

French, J. P. R, & Raven, B. (1959). The bases of social power. In D. Cartwright (ed.), *Studies in social power* (pp. 150–165). Ann Arbor, MI: Institute for Social Research.

Frey, L. R., & Barge, J. K. (eds). (1997). *Managing group life: Communication in decision-making groups*. Boston: Prentice Hall.

Furman, W., & Buhrmester, D. (1985). Children's perceptions of the personal relationship in their social networks. *Developmental Psychology, 21*, 1016–1024.

Furstenberg, F. F., Jr., & Harris, K. M. (1993). When and why fathers matter: Impacts of father involvement on the children of adolescent mothers. In R. I. Lerman & T. J. Ooms (eds), *Young unwed fathers: Changing roles and emerging policies* (pp. 117–138). Philadelphia: Temple University Press.

Galvin, K. M., Bylund, C. L., & Brommel, B. J. (2008). *Family communication: Cohesion & change* (7th edn). Boston: Allyn & Bacon.

Gardner, K. A., & Cutrona, C. E. (2004). Social support communication in families. In A. L. Vangelisti (ed.), *Handbook of family communication* (pp. 495–512). Mahwah, NJ: Lawrence Erlbaum.

Gibb, J. (1961). Defensive communication. *Journal of Communication, 11*, 141–148.

Gillham, J. E., Reivich, K. J., Jaycox, L. H., & Seligman, M. E. P. (1995). Prevention of depressive symptoms in school children: Two year follow up study. *Psychological Science, 6*, 343–351.

Gleason, J. B. (ed.). (1993). *The development of language* (3rd edn). New York: Macmillan.

Golish, T. D., & Caughlin, J. P. (2002). "I'd rather not talk about it": Adolescents' and young adults' use of topic avoidance in stepfamilies. *Journal of Applied Communication Research, 30*(1), 78–106.

Goodman, C. C., & Silverstein, M. (2001). Grandmothers who parent their grandchildren: An exploratory study of close relations across three generations. *Journal of Family Issues, 22*(5), 557–578.

Gopnik, A., Meltzoff, A. N., & Kuhl, P. K. (1999). *The scientist in the crib: What early learning tells us about the mind*. NY: HarperCollins Publisher.

Gottman, J. G. (1994). *What predicts divorce: The relationship between marital processes and marital outcomes*. Hillsdale, NJ: Lawrence Erlbaum.

Gottman, J. M. (1990). Children of gay and lesbian parents. *Marriage and Family Review, 14*, 177–196.

Gottman, J., Declaire, J., & Goleman, D. (1998). *Raising an emotionally intelligent child*. New York: Simon & Schuster.

Grace, G. (2008). Changes in the classification and framing of education in Britain, 1950s to 2000s: An interpretive essay after Bernstein. *Journal of Educational Administration and History, 40* (3), 209–220.

Green, R., Mandel, J. B., Hotvedt, M. E., Gray, J., & Smith, L. (1986). Lesbian mothers and their children: A comparison with solo parent heterosexual mothers and their children. *Archives of Sexual Behavior, 15*, 167–184.

References

Grieser, D. L., & Kuhl, P. K. (1988). Maternal speech to infants in a tonal language: Support for universal prosodic features in motherese. *Developmental Psychology, 24*(1), 14–20.

Hamilton, B. E., Martin, J. A., & Ventura, S. J. (2009). Births: Preliminary Data for 2007. *National Vital Statistics Reports, 57* (12). US Department of Health and Human Services, Centers for Disease Control and Prevention. Retrieved November 21, 2009: http://www.cdc.gov/nchs/births.htm.

Harris, J. R. (1998). *The nurture assumption: Why children turn out the way they do.* New York: Free Press.

Hartup, W. W. (1985). Relationships and their significance in cognitive development. In R. A. Hinde, A. Perret-Clermot, & J. Stevenson-Hinde (eds), *Social relationships and cognitive development* (pp. 66–82). New York: Oxford University Press.

Harwood, J. (2000). Communicative predictors of solidarity in the grandparent-grandchild relationship. *Journal of Social and Personal Relationships, 17*(6), 743–766. Harwood, J. (2004). Relational, role, and social identity as expressed in grandparents' personal web sites. *Communication Studies, 55,* 268–286.

Haslett, B. (1983). Preschoolers' communicative strategies in gaining compliance from peers: A developmental study. *Quarterly Journal of Speech, 69,* 84–99.

Haslett, B., & Samter, W. (1997). *Children communicating: The first five years.* Mahwah, NJ: Lawrence Erlbaum.

Hatfield, S. R., & Abrams, L. J. (1995). Interaction between fathers and their children in traditional and single-father families: A multimethod exploration. In T. J. Socha & G. H. Stamp (eds), *Parents, children and communication: Frontiers of theory and research* (pp. 103–112). Mahwah, NJ: Lawrence Erlbaum.

Hazen, C., & Shaver, P. (1987). Romantic love conceptualized as an attachment process. *Journal of Personality and Social Psychology, 52,* 511–524.

Hecht, M. L., & Miller-Day, M. (2009). Drug resistance strategies project: Using narrative theory to enhance adolescents' communicative competence. In L. R. Frey & K. N. Cissna (eds), *Routledge handbook of applied communication research* (pp. 535–557). New York: Routledge.

Heywood, C. (2001). *A history of childhood.* Cambridge, UK: Polity.

Hickey, T., Hickey, L., & Kalish, R. A. (1968). Children's perceptions of the elderly. *Journal of Genetic Psychology, 112,* 227–235.

Hinde, R. A., & Stevenson-Hinde, J. (eds), *Relationships within families: Mutual influences* (pp. 168–180). Oxford, UK: Oxford University Press.

Hirokawa, R. Y., & Salazar, A. J. (1997). An integrated approach to communication and group decision-making. In L. Frey & J. K. Barge (eds), *Managing group life: Communication in decision-making groups* (pp. 156–181). Boston: Houghton Mifflin.

Hobbs, R. (1997). Literacy for the information age. In J. Flood, S. B. Heath, & D. Papp (eds), *Handbook of research on teaching literacy through the communicative and visual arts* (pp. 7–14). New York: Macmillan.

References

Hoff-Ginsberg, E. (1991). Mother–child conversation in different social classes and communicative settings. *Child Development, 62,* 782–796.

Holladay, S., & Seipke, H. L. (2003, November). *Communication between grandparents and grandchildren in geographically dispersed relationships.* Paper presented at the annual meeting of the National Communication Association, Miami, FL.

Hopper, R., & Naremore, R. C. (1978). *Children's speech: A practical guide to communication development.* New York: Harper & Row.

Humphrey, T. (1978). Function of the nervous system during prenatal life. In U. Stave (ed.), *Perinatal physiology* (pp. 651–683). New York: Plenum.

Infante, D. A., & Rancer, A. S. (1982). A conceptualization and measure of argumentativeness. *Journal of Personality Assessment, 46,* 72–80.

Infante, D. A., Chandler, T. A., & Rudd, J. E. (1989). Test of an argumentative skill deficiency model of interspousal violence. *Communication Monographs, 56,* 163–177.

Infante, D. A., & Wigley, C. J. III (1986). Verbal aggressiveness: An interpersonal model and measure. *Communication Monographs, 53,* 61–69.

Johnson, W. (2000). *Parenting and providing: The impact of parents' fair share on paternal involvement.* New York: Manpower Demonstration Research Corporation.

Jones, C., & Adamson, L. (1987). Language use in mother–child and mother–child–sibling interactions. *Child Development, 58,* 356–366.

Juroe, D. J., & Juroe, B. B. (1983). *Successful stepparenting.* Old Tappan, NJ: F. H. Revell.

Kahn, R. L., & Antonucci, T. C. (1980). Convoys over the life course: Attachment, roles and social support. In P. B. Baltes & O. C. Brim (eds), *Life-span, development, and behavior* (pp. 254–283). New York: Academic Press.

Kahneman, D., & Tversky, A. (1979). Prospect theory: An analysis of decision under risk. *Econometrica, 47,* 263–291.

Kaiser Foundation (2005). *Generation M: Media in the lives of 8–18 year-olds: Executive summary.* Retrieved July 21, 2009 from http://www.kff.org/entmedia/upload/Executive-Summary-Generation-M-Media-in-the-Lives-of-8–18-Year-olds.pdf

Keepin' it Real (2009). Retrieved July 21, 2009 from http://keepinitreal.asu.edu/.

Keller, H., Scholmerich, A., & Eibl-Eibesfeldt, I. (1988). Communication patterns in adult–infant interactions in Western and non-Western cultures. *Journal of Cross-Cultural Psychology, 19*(4), 427–445.

Kelly, G. A. (1969–1979). The autobiography of a theory. In B. Maher (ed.), *Clinical psychology and personality: The collected papers of George Kelly* (pp. 46–65). New York: Wiley. [Original work published 1969].

Kilmann, R., & Thomas, K. (1975). Interpersonal conflict handling behavior as reflections of Jungian personality dimensions. *Psychology Reports, 37,* 971–980.

Kornhaber, A., & Woodward, K. L. (1981). *Grandparents/grandchildren: The vital connection*. Garden City, NY: Anchor Press/Doubleday.

Kozol, J. (1992). *Savage inequalities: Children in American schools*. New York: HarperPerennial.

Krashen, S. (1973). Lateralization, language learning, and the critical period: Some new evidence. *Language Learning, 23*, 63–74.

Kubey, R., & Csikszentmihalyi, M. (1990). *Television and the quality of life: How viewing shapes everyday experience*. Hillsdale, NJ: Lawrence Erlbaum.

Lacina, J. (2007). Computers and young children. *Childhood Education*. Retrieved Jun 24, 2009 from http://www.thefreelibrary.com/Computers+and+young+childrena0172907444.

Lamb, M. E. (1987). *The father's role*, Hillsdale, NJ: Lawrence Erlbaum.

Langer, S. K. (1972). *Mind: An essay on human feeling* (Vol. II). Baltimore: Johns Hopkins University Press.

Langlois, A., Baken, R. J., & Wilder, C. N. (1980). Pre-speech respiratory behavior during the first year of life. In T. Murry & J. Murry (eds), *Infant communication: Cry and early speech* (pp. 56–84). Houston, TX: College-Hill Press.

Le Poire, B. (2005). *Family communication: Nurturing and control in a changing world*. Thousand Oaks, CA: Sage.

Lecanuet, J. P., Granier-Deferre, C., Jacquet, A. Y., Capponi, I., & Ledru, L. (1993). Prenatal discrimination of a male and a female voice uttering the same sentence. *Early Development and Parenting, 2* (4), 217–228.

Lecours, A. R. (1975). Myelogenetic correlates of the development of speech and language. In E. H. Lenneberg & E. Lenneberg (eds), *Foundations of language development: A multidisciplinary approach* (Vol. I, pp. 121–135). New York: Academic Press.

Lenneberg, E. (1967). *Biological foundations of language*. New York: Wiley.

Levasseur, M. (2007). *Familiar with tweens? You should be . . . The Quebec Source on Global Trends in Tourism*. Retrieved June 15, 2009 from http://tourismintelligence.ca/2007/02/09/familiar-with-tweens-you-should-be/?tagged=

Lewin, K. & Lippitt, R. (1938). An experimental approach to the study of autocracy and democracy: A preliminary note. *Sociometry, 1*, 292–300.

Lewis, J. M., Johnson-Reitz, L., & Wallerstein, J. S. (2004). Communication in divorced and single-parent families. In A. Vangelisti (ed.), *Handbook of family communication* (pp. 197–214). Mahwah, NJ: Lawrence Erlbaum.

Licht, B., Simoni, H., & Perrig-Chiello, P. (2008). Conflict between peers in infancy and toddler age: What do they fight about? Early Years: An International Journal of Research and Development, 28, 235–249

Lin, M. C., & Harwood, J. (2003). Predictors of grandparent-grandchild relational solidarity in Taiwan. *Journal of Social and Personal Relationships, 20*, 537–563.

MacDermid, S. M., Huston, T. D., & McHale, S. M. (1990). Changes in marriage associates with the transition to parenthood: Individual differences as a function of sex-role attitudes and changes in the division of household labor. *Journal of Marriage and the Family, 52*(2), 475–486.

McKay, V. C. (1993). Making connections: Narrative as the expression of continuity between generations of grandparents and grandchildren. In N. Coupland & J. F. Nussbaum (eds), *Discourse and lifespan identity* (pp. 173–185). Newbury Park, CA: Sage.

McLanahan, S., & Sandefur, G. (1994). *Growing up with a single parent: What hurts, what helps.* Cambridge, MA: Harvard University Press.

McLuhan, M. (1962). *The Gutenberg galaxy: The making of typographic man.* Toronto: University of Toronto Press.

Mannle, S., & Tomasello, M. (1987). Fathers, siblings, and the bridge hypothesis. In K. E. Nelson & A. van Kleeck (eds), *Children's language* (Vol. 6) (pp. 23–42). Hillsdale, NJ: Lawrence Erlbaum.

Masten, A. S., & Reed, M. G. J. (2002). Resilience in development. In. C. R. Synder & S. J. Lopez (eds), *The handbook of positive psychology* (pp. 74–88). New York: Oxford University Press.

Mebert, C. J. (1991). Variability in the transition to parenthood experience. In K. Pillemer & K. McCartney (eds), *Parent–child relations throughout life* (pp. 43–57). Hillsdale, NJ: Lawrence Erlbaum.

Messer, D. J. (1994). *The development of communication: From social interaction to language.* West Sussex, UK: Wiley.

Meyer v. State of Nebraska, 262 US 392 (1925).

Meyrowitz, J. (1998). Multiple media literacies. *Journal of Communication, 48*, 96–108.

Mishel, W., Shoda, Y., & Rodriguez, M. L. (1989). Delay of gratification in children. *Science, 244*, 933–938.

Moerk, E. (1974). Changes in verbal child-mother interactions with increasing language skills of 3-year-old children in relation to social class. *Applied Psycholinguistics 15*(3), 371–394.

National Communication Association (1998). K-*12 speaking, listening, and media literacy standards and competency statements.* Washington, DC: National Communication Association. Available at http://www.natcom.org/nca/files/ccLibraryFiles/FILENAME/000000000119/K12%20Standards.pdf.

Nord, C. W., & Zill, N. (1996). *Non-custodial parents' participation in their children's lives: Evidence from the Survey of Income and Program Participation.* Washington, DC: US Department of Health and Human Services.

Nussbaum, J. F., Pecchioni, L. L., Robinson, J. D., & Thompson, T. L. (2000). *Communication and aging* (2nd edn). Mahwah, NJ: Lawrence Erlbaum.

Olson, D. H., Russell, C., & Sprenkle, D. (eds). (1983). *Circumplex model: Systematic assessment and treatment of families.* New York: Hayworth Press.

Ong, W. J. (1967). *The presence of the word: Some prolegomena for cultural and religious history.* Minneapolis: University of Minnesota Press.

References

Ong, W. J. (1982). *Orality and literacy: The technologizing of the word*. London: Routledge.

Oshima-Takane, Y., Goodz, E., & Derevensky, J. L. (1996). Birth order effects on early language development: Do secondborn children learn from overheard speech? *Child Development, 67*, 621–634.

Oxford English Dictionary (2009). Oxford, UK: Oxford University Press. Retrieved May 26, 2009, from http://dictionary.oed.com/.

Paikoff, R. L., & Brooks-Gunn, J. (1991). Do parent–child relationships change during puberty? *Psychological Bulletin, 110*, 47–66.

Palfrey, J. & Gasser, U. (2008). *Born digital: Understanding the first generation of digital natives*. New York: Basic Books.

Parke, R. D., & Sawain D. B. (1981). Father–infant interaction in the newborn period: A re-evaluation of some current myths. In E. M. Hetherington & R. D. Parke (eds), *Contemporary readings in child psychology* (2nd edn, pp. 229–234). New York: McGraw-Hill.

Patrick, D., & Paladino, J. (2009). The community interactions of gay and lesbian foster parents. In T. J. Socha & G. H. Stamp (eds), *Parents and children communicating with society: Managing relationships outside of home* (pp. 323–342). New York: Routledge.

Patterson, G. R. (1979). A performance theory for coercive family interaction. In R. B. Cairns (ed.), *The analysis of social interactions* (pp. 119–162). Hillsdale, NJ: Lawrence Erlbaum.

Pavlov, I. P. (1928–1941). *Lectures on conditioned reflexes* (Vols. I & II, W. H. Gantt, Trans.) New York: International Publishers.

Pecchioni, L. L., & Croghan, J. M. (2002). Young adults' stereotypes of older adults with their grandparents as the targets. *Journal of Communication, 52*(4), 715–730.

Penn Resiliency Program (2009). Resilience research in children. Retrieved July 21, 2009, from http://www.ppc.sas.upenn.edu/prpsum.htm.

Percy, W. (1954). *The message in the bottle*. New York: Farrar, Straus, & Giroux.

Perlman, M., Garfinkel, D. A., & Turrell, S. L. (2007). Parent and sibling influences on the quality of children's conflict behaviours across the preschool period. *Social Development, 16*, 619–641.

Peterson, C. (2006). *A primer in positive psychology*. Oxford UK: Oxford University Press.

Peterson, C., & Seligman, M. E. P. (2004). *Character strengths and virtues: A handbook and classification*. Oxford and New York: Oxford University Press.

Petronio, S., Reeder, H. M., Hecht, M. L., & Ros-Mendoza, T. M. (1996). Disclosure of sexual abuse by children and adolescents. *Journal of Applied Communication Research, 24*(3), 181–199.

Piaget, J. (1959). *The language and thought of the child*. London: Routledge & Kegan Paul.

References

Planalp, S. (1999). *Communication emotion: Social, moral, and cultural processes*. Cambridge, UK: Cambridge University Press.

Postman, N. (1985). *Amusing ourselves to death: Public discourse in the age of show business*. New York: Penguin.

Pulakos, J. (1987). The effect of birth order on perceived family roles. *Individual Psychology, 43*, 319–328.

Rabain-Jamin, J. (1989). Culture and early social interactions: The example of mother-infant object play in African and native French families. *European Journal of Psychology and Education, 4*(2), 295–305.

Rathunde, K., & Csikszentmihalyi, M. (1991). Adolescent happiness and family interaction. In K. A. Pillemer & K. McCartney (eds), *Parent–child relationships throughout life* (pp. 143–161). Hillsdale, NJ: Lawrence Erlbaum.

Reid, J. S. (1986). Social interactional patterns in families of abused and non-abused children. In C. Zahn-Waxler, E. M. Cummings, & R. Iannotti (eds), *Altruism and aggression: Biological and social origins* (pp. 238–257). Cambridge, UK: Cambridge University Press.

Reynolds, T. J. (2005). Lifegoals: The development of a decision-making curriculum for education. *Journal of Public Policy and Marketing, 24*, 75–81.

Richman, A. L., Miller, P. M., & LeVine, R. A. (1992). Cultural and educational variations in maternal responsiveness. *Developmental Psychology, 28*(4), 614–621.

Roberto, A. J., Carlyle, K. E., Goodall, C. E., & Castle, J. D. (2009). The relationship between parents' verbal aggressiveness and responsiveness and young adult children's attachment style and relational satisfaction with parents. *Journal of Family Communication, 9*, 90–106.

Roberts, D. F., Foehr, U. G., Rideout, V. J., & Brodie, M. (1999) *Kids and media @ the new millennium*. Menlo Park, CA: Kaiser Family Foundation. http://www.kff.org.

Robertson, J. F. (1977). Grandmotherhood: A study of role conceptions. *Journal of Marriage and Family, 39*, 165–174.

Rodgers, J. L., Cleveland, H. H., van den Oord, E., & Rosenberg, M. B. (2005). *Raising children compassionately: Parenting the nonviolent communication way*. Encinitas, CA: PuddleDancer Press.

Rowe, D. C. (2000). Resolving the debate over birth order, family size, and intelligence. *American Psychologist, 55*(6), 599–612.

Saluter, A. F. (1996). *Marital status and living arrangements: March 1994. US Bureau of the Census, current population reports* (Series P20–484). Washington, DC: US Government Printing Office.

Satir, V. (1972). *Peoplemaking*. Palo Alto, CA: Science and Behavior Books.

Satir, V. (1988). *The new peoplemaking*. Mountain View, CA: Science and Behavior Books.

References

Savage, L. J. (1954). *The foundations of statistics.* New York: Wiley.

Scaife, M., & Bruner, J. S. (1975). The capacity for joint attention in the infant. *Nature, 253,* 265–266.

Schaefer, E. S. (1959). A circumplex model for maternal behavior. *Journal of Abnormal and Social Psychology, 59,* 226–235.

Schaefer, E. S. (1997). Integration of configurational and factorial models for family relationships and child behavior. In R. Plutchik & H. R. Conte (eds), *Circumplex models of personality and emotions* (pp. 133–153). Washington, DC: American Psychological Association.

Scheerhorn, D., & Geist, P. (1997). Social dynamics in groups. In L. R. Frey & J. K. Barge (eds), *Managing group life: Communication in decision-making groups* (pp. 81–103). Boston: Prentice Hall.

Schrodt, P., Baxter, L. A., McBride, C., Braithwaite, D. O., & Fine, M. A. (2006). The divorce decree, communication, and the structuration of coparenting relationships in stepfamilies. *Journal of Social and Personal Relationships, 23* (5), 741–459.

Segel, U. A, & Mayadas, N. S. (2005). Assessment of issues facing immigrant and refugee families. *Child Welfare, 84* (5), 563–583.

Segrin, C., Hanzal, A., & Domschke, T. J. (2009). Accuracy and bias in newly-wed couples' perceptions of conflict styles and the association with marital satisfaction. *Communication Monographs, 76,* 207–233.

Seligman, M. E. P. (2002). *Authentic happiness.* New York: Free Press.

Selman, R. L. (1980). *The growth of interpersonal understanding: Developmental and clinical analyses.* New York: Academic Press.

Shimanoff, S. (1980). *Communication rules: Theory and research.* Beverly Hills, CA: Sage.

Shore, R. J., & Hayslip, B., Jr. (1995). Custodial grandparenting: Implications for children's development. In A. E. Gottfried & A. W. Gottfried (eds), *Redefining families: Implications for children's development* (pp. 171–218). New York: Plenum.

Shotter, J. (1993). *Cultural politics of everyday life.* Toronto: University of Toronto Press.

Skinner, B. F. (1974). *About behaviorism.* New York: Knopf.

Smiley, P., & Huttenlocher, J. (1989). Young children's acquisition of emotion concepts. In C. Saarni, & P. L. Harris (eds), *Children's understanding of emotion* (pp. 270–298). New York: Springer-Verlag.

Snow, M., Jacklin, C., & Maccoby, E. (1983). Sex-of-child differences in father–child interaction at one year of age. *Child Development, 54,* 227–232.

Snyder, C. R., & Lopez, S. J. (2007). *Positive psychology: The scientific and practical explorations of human strengths.* Thousand Oaks, CA: Sage.

Socha, T. J. (1999). Communication in family units: Studying the first group. In L. Frey, D. Gouran, & M. S. Poole (eds), *The handbook of group communication theory & research* (pp. 475–492). Thousand Oaks, CA: Sage.

References

Socha, T. J. (2006). Orchestrating and directing domestic potential through communication: Towards a Positive Reframing of "Discipline." In L. Turner & R. West (eds), *Family communication: A reference for theory and research* (pp. 219–236). Thousand Oaks, CA: Sage.

Socha, T. J. (2009). Family as agency of potential: Toward a positive ontology of applied family communication theory and research. In L. Frey & K. Cissna (eds), *Handbook of applied communication* (pp. 309–330). New York: Routledge.

Socha, T. J., & Diggs, R. C. (eds) (1999). *Communication, race, & family: Exploring communication in Black, White, and Biracial families*. Mahwah, NJ: Lawrence Erlbaum.

Socha, T. J., & Pitts, M. (eds). (in review). *The positive side of interpersonal communication*. [Proposal for edited volume.]

Socha, T. J., & Socha, D. M. (1994). Children's task group communication: Did we learn it all in kindergarten? In L Frey (ed.), *Group communication in context: Studies of natural groups* (pp. 227–246). Hillsdale, NJ: Lawrence Erlbaum.

Socha, T. J., & Stamp, G. H. (eds). (1995). *Parents, children, and communication: Frontiers of theory and research*. Mahwah, NJ: Lawrence Erlbaum.

Socha, T. J., & Stamp, G. H. (eds). (2009). *Parents and children communicating with society: Managing relationships outside of home*. New York: Routledge.

Solomon, J. C., & Marx, J. (1995). "To grandmother's house we go": Health and school adjustment of children raised solely by grandparents. *The Gerontologist, 35*(3), 386–394.

Stansbury, V. K., & Coll, K. M. (1998). Myers-Briggs attitude typology: The influence of birth order with other family variables. *Family Journal, 6*(2), 116–122.

Stern, D. N. (1977). *The first relationship*. Cambridge, UK: Cambridge University Press.

Stern, D. N., Jaffe, J., Beebe, B., & Bennett, S. L. (1975). Vocalizing in unison and in alternation: Two modes of communication within the mother-infant dyad. *Annals of the New York Academy of Sciences: Developmental Psycholinguistics and Communication Disorders, 263*, 89–100.

Sternberg, R. J. (1986). A triangular theory of love. *Psychological Review, 93*, 119–135.

Sulloway, F. J. (2001). Birth order, sibling competition, and human behavior. In P. S. Davies & H. R. Holcolmb (eds), *Conceptual challenges in evolutionary psychology: Innovative research strategies* (pp. 39–83). Dordrecht & Boston: Kluwer Academic Publishers.

Toda, S., Fogel, A., & Kawai, M. (1990). Maternal speech to three-month-old infants in the United States and Japan. *Journal of Child Language 17*, 270–294.

References

Turner, E. K. (2008). Learning how to fight: Connections between conflict resolution patterns in marital and sibling relationships. *Dissertation Abstracts International*, 68 (11-B), 7680.

Turner, L. H., & West, R. (2002). *Perspectives on family communication* (2nd edn). Boston: McGraw-Hill.

UNICEF (2009). [United Nations Children's Fund website.] Retrieved May 20, 2009, from http://www.unicef.org/.

United States Census Bureau (2008). Table C3. Living arrangements of children under 18 years/1 and marital status of parents, by age, sex, race, and Hispanic origin/2 and selected characteristics of the child for all children: 2008. Retrieved November 21, 2009: http://www.census.gov/population/www.socdemo/hh-fam/cps2008.html.

United States Department of Agriculture (2009). Cost of raising a child calculator. Retrieved June 15, 2009 from http://www.cnpp.usda.gov/calculatorintro.htm.

Valsiner, J. (1989). Organization of children's social development in polygamic families. In J. Valsiner (ed.), *Child development in cultural context* (pp. 67–85). Toronto: Hogrefe and Huber.

Van Evra, J. (2004). *Television and child development*. Mahwah, NJ: Lawrence Erlbaum.

Vogl-Bauer, S. (2009). When the world comes home: Examining internal and external influences on communication exchanges between parents and their boomerang children. In T. J. Socha, & G. H. Stamp (eds), *Parents and children communicating with society: Managing relationships outside of home* (pp. 285–304). New York: Routledge.

Vygotsky, L. S. (1978). *Mind in society: The development of higher psychological processes*. Cambridge, MA: Harvard University Press.

Vygotsky, L. S. (1986). Thought and language (Alex Kozulin, Trans.). Cambridge, MA: MIT Press. [Original work published 1934.]

Warren, C. (1995). Parent–child communication about sex. In T. J. Socha & G. H. Stamp (eds), *Parents, children, and communication: Frontiers of theory and research* (pp. 173–201). Mahwah, NJ: Lawrence Erlbaum.

Warren, R. M., & Ackroff, J. M. (1976). Two types of auditory sequence perception. *Perception and Psychophysics*, 20, 387–394.

Wartella, E. A., Lee, J. H., & Caplovitz, A. G. (Nov., 2002). *Children and interactive media: Research compendium update*. Retrieved July 27, 2009 from http://www.markle.org/downloadable_assets/cimcomp_update.pdf.

Wartella, E. A., O'Keefe, B., & Scantlin, R. (May, 2000). *Children and interactive media: A compendium of current research and directions for the future*. A report to the Markle Foundation. Available at: http://www.markle.org/downloadable_assets/cimcompendium.pdf.

Wegscheider, S. (1981). *Another chance: Hope and health for the alcoholic family*. Palo Alto, CA: Science & Behavior Books.

References

Weintraub-Austin, E., Hust, S. J. T., & Kistler, M. E. (2009). Arming parents with strategies to affect children's interactions with commercial interests. In T. J. Socha, & G. H. Stamp (eds), *Parents and children communicating with society: Managing relationships outside of home* (pp. 215–240). New York: Routledge.

Wertsch, J. V. (1979). The regulation of human action and the given-new organization of private speech. In G. Zivin (ed.), *The development of self-regulation through private speech* (pp. 79–98). New York: Wiley.

Weston, K. (1991). *Families we choose: Lesbians, gays, kinship*. New York: Columbia University Press.

Whalen, S. (1999). Challenging play and the cultivation of talent: Lessons from the Key School's flow activities room. In N. Colangelo & S. Assouline (eds), *Talent development III* (pp. 409–411). Scottsdale, AZ: Gifted Psychology Press.

Wilson, B. J. (2004). The mass media and family communication. In A. Vangelisti (ed.), *Handbook of family communication* (pp. 563–501). Mahwah, NJ: Lawrence Erlbaum.

Wilson, S. R., Shi, X., Tirmenstein, L., Norris, A., Rack, J. J. (2006). Parental physical negative touch and child noncompliance in abusive, neglectful, and comparison families. In L. H. Turner & R. West (eds), *The family communication sourcebook* (pp. 237–258). Thousand Oaks, CA: Sage.

Wood, B. S. (1981). *Children and communication: Verbal and nonverbal language development*. Englewood Cliffs, NJ: Prentice Hall.

Wood, J. T. (2000). *Relational communication: Continuity and change in personal relationships* (2nd edn). Belmont, CA: Wadsworth Publishing Company.

Wood, V. (1982, Winter). Grandparenthood: An ambiguous role. *Generations: Journal of the Western Gerontological Society, 22*, 18–24.

Yingling, J. (1981). *Temporal features of infant speech: A description of babbling patterns circumscribed by postural achievement*. Unpublished doctoral dissertation, University of Denver.

Yingling, J. (1984, May). *Infant speech timing: The development of individual control*. Paper presented at the International Communication Association convention, San Francisco.

Yingling, J. (1990/1991). "Does that mean 'no'?" Negotiating proto-conversation in infant–caregiver pairs. *Research on Language and Social Interaction, 24*, 71–108.

Yingling, J. (2004). *A lifetime of communication: Transformations through relational dialogues*. Mahwah, NJ: Lawrence Erlbaum.

Author Index

Subject Index